D1561768

The
Prudential Presidency

The
Prudential Presidency

An Aristotelian Approach to
Presidential Leadership

Ethan M. Fishman
Foreword by Erwin C. Hargrove

Westport, Connecticut
London

Library of Congress Cataloging-in-Publication Data

Fishman, Ethan M.
    The prudential presidency : an Aristotelian approach to presidential leadership /
    Ethan M. Fishman ; foreword by Erwin C. Hargrove.
        p. cm.
    Includes bibliographical references and index.
    ISBN 0–275–97111–2 (alk. paper)
    1. Presidents—United States—History.   2. Political leadership—United States—
    History.   I. Title.
    JK511.F57   2001
    973'.09'9—dc21   00–058020

British Library Cataloguing in Publication Data is available.

Library of Congress Catalog Card Number: 00–058020
ISBN: 0–275–97111–2

First published in 2001

Praeger Publishers, 88 Post Road West, Westport, CT 06881
An imprint of Greenwood Publishing Group, Inc.
www.praeger.com

Printed in the United States of America

The paper used in this book complies with the
Permanent Paper Standard issued by the National
Information Standards Organization (Z39.48–1984).

10 9 8 7 6 5 4 3 2 1

Copyright Acknowledgments

The author and publisher gratefully acknowledge permission for use of the following material:

Ethan Fishman, " 'Falling Back' on Natural Law and Prudence: A Reply to Souryal and Potts," *Journal of Criminal Justice Education* 5, no. 2 (1994): 189–203. Reprinted with Permission of the Academy of Criminal Justice Sciences.

Ethan Fishman, " 'Applied Idealism': Theodore Roosevelt's Prudent Approach to Conservation," *Theodore Roosevelt Association Journal* 22, no. 3 (1998): 3–7. Reprinted with permission of the Theodore Roosevelt Association.

Ethan Fishman "Under the Circumstances: Abraham Lincoln and Classical Prudence" in *Abraham Lincoln: Sources and Styles of Leadership*, ed. Frank J. Williams, William D. Pederson, and Vincent J. Marsala (Greenwood Press, 1994). Copyright © 1994 Frank J. Williams, William D. Pederson, and Vincent J. Marsala. Reproduced with permission of Greenwood Publishing Group, Inc., Westport, CT.

Ethan Fishman, "The Prudential FDR" in *FDR and the Modern Presidency*, ed. Mark J. Rozell and William D. Pederson (Praeger, 1997). Copyright © 1997 Mark J. Rozell and William D. Pederson. Reproduced with the permission of Greenwood Publishing Group, Inc., Westport, CT.

TO MY CHILDREN,
ZOE AND BRENNER

Contents

Foreword

Erwin C. Hargrove

Politicians who describe themselves as realists wish to see the world as it is and are too often willing to relax their goals if they appear unobtainable. Idealists, on the other hand, hope that their commitment will alter what appears to be intractable reality. Pragmatists do not so much seek an efficient balance between means and ends as an agreement that will temporarily reduce conflict without consideration of any ultimate goal. And self-serving politicians will use the rhetoric of realism, idealism, and pragmatism to manipulate others in their own behalf.

These comparisons reveal that the scope of political agreement and disagreement is complex and not easily captured in models of political behavior. We must understand the psychological worlds that inhabit the minds of politicians in action. It is not enough to categorize their actions and infer purposes from their behavior. It is even less warranted to impose a paradigm that sees their purposes as the attainment of objectives that the paradigm attributes to them. The theory of the firm may, or may not, be able to predict what firms will do as objective circumstances change. And attempts to transplant that approach into political science so as to predict action based on attributed stakes and changing situations are sure to fail because the scope is too limited. We must know the phenomenological world of the politician in all its richness.

A Buddhist saying makes my point: "If the string is too tight, it will snap. But if it is too loose, the instrument will not play." How is one to achieve a balance between the good and the possible that is realistic but also attainable? Ethan Fishman takes us a good part of the way in his answers to this question.

He takes his understanding of the best political action from Aristotle and the idea of *phronesis* or prudence. Practical reason and judgment, for Aristotle, contain two separate elements: knowledge of the relation of means to ends and a commitment to and understanding of moral purpose. One cannot properly exist without the other. The good politician and the good person must be one and the same. Political skill, without moral goodness, is sterile. And good character, without the craft of politics, is ineffective. Fishman gives us the point-counterpoint comparisons of prudence with idealism, pragmatism, and cynicism and thus opens up the political world to all its possibilities.

Aristotle and Plato were closer than some may think in their shared insistence on the reality of the moral life. But Plato put his hope in wise guardians who would lead the unwashed into habits of goodness and direct the society at the same time. Aristotle did not have much use for governance strictly from theories or abstractions. He believed we are better guided by experience and practical reason in given cases. As Justice Oliver Wendell Holmes said, the life of the law is not knowledge but experience.

Only prudence, in Aristotle's sense, captures the elastic balance between means and ends because it actively seeks that balance and other political modes of thought do not. Fishman gives us illustrations of the deal-making pragmatist, the naive idealist, and the cynical realist through a number of case studies of presidential leadership. Abraham Lincoln and Franklin Roosevelt are exemplars of practical reason because they knew how to combine the necessities of politics with moral agency. When Lincoln wrote Horace Greeley that his goal was to save the Union and that he would abolish slavery or keep it, whichever would save the Union, he was acting as a practical politician. And the Emancipation Proclamation itself, which only freed some of the slaves, was practical politics. But the rhetoric of the Gettysburg Address and the Second Inaugural Address revealed a Lincoln who created a new political prose of moral purpose for the nation derived from the Declaration of Independence. By the same token, FDR sought reform, not against capitalism, but as a means of saving it. He would not nationalize the banks, as idealistic advisors suggested, but he would regulate business in new ways. On the other hand, the often topsy-turvy politics of the New Deal gave us plenty of short term, pragmatic remedies without coherence of plan or purpose.

Woodrow Wilson and Jimmy Carter were subject to a naive idealism that undercut their own purposes. The failure of the United States to join the League of Nations and the difficulty a moralistic Carter encountered when trying to work his way with congressional politicians are illustrations of idealism without the spine of realistic calculation. Harry Truman's decision to drop the atomic bomb, John Kennedy's fear of disbanding the Cuban invasion force that was to flounder at the Bay of Pigs, and Bill Clinton's surrender to a "don't ask, don't tell" policy about gays in the military all reveal pragmatism as an end in itself without reflection about possible alternatives. Richard Nixon's cynical belief that "dirty tricks" are the norm of politics destroyed his presidency, and the lack of credibility in many of Clinton's political promises surely undercut his ability to create coalitions for action.

Fishman directs us to and builds upon a recently developed literature about practical reason in politics, which is necessarily a literature about political leadership. As Aristotle wrote, citizens need not be prudent but political leaders must be so. Citizens know whether or not the policy meets their needs but they cannot be expected to know how to join ends and means. That is the task of leaders. Students of political theory have developed these ideas, but Fishman has taken a most valuable first step in his efforts to connect what we think about politics to what we do in politics. This is a breath of fresh air after so much attention has been given to how political actors seek only tangible stakes according to stipulated conditions. The theory of the firm is not a theory for politics.

Acknowledgments

I am grateful to William Pederson of the Louisiana State University at Shreveport, the talented and tireless coordinator of a series of conferences on the great American presidents that has been held on his campus every three years since its inception in 1992. By inviting me to share my ideas about the relationship between Aristotle's political philosophy and presidential leadership with conference participants, Professor Pederson played a significant role in facilitating the development of this book.

I am also indebted to Erwin Hargrove of Vanderbilt University. Professor Hargrove read the entire manuscript, made some excellent recommendations for its improvement, and graciously contributed a foreword. Had I followed his advice more closely, my effort would have been a much stronger one.

Others who read the manuscript and provided helpful comments to me on how to enhance its meaning are Sue Fishman, Professor Mark Rozell of Catholic University, Professor Sam Fisher of the University of South Alabama, and Professor Voorhees Dunn of Kingsborough Community College of the City University of New York.

Chief among those who supplied me with the necessary encouragement to see the project through to completion are Sidney Fishman, Gene Sullivan and Matt Rhodes. By far the most enthusiastic support came from my children, Zoe Fishman and Brenner Fishman. It is with a great deal of love and pride that I dedicate *The Prudential Presidency* to them.

_____ CHAPTER 1 _____

Introduction

During the 1998–99 congressional impeachment hearings a general consensus appeared to exist among Bill Clinton's supporters and detractors alike that his personal behavior was detrimental both to the presidency and to the nation. Senator Joseph Lieberman seemed to speak for many of his colleagues when he accused the president of engaging in transgressions involving deceit, abuse of power, and contempt for the law that have had a devastating impact on the credibility of the executive branch and the moral foundations of American democracy. "I am afraid that the misconduct the president has admitted may be reinforcing one of the worst messages being delivered by our popular culture, which is that values are fungible," Lieberman claimed (Duffy and Walsh 1998, 16).

Whether or not they considered Clinton's actions to be impeachable, in short, and contrary to Clinton's own repeated protestations, Lieberman and many of his colleagues were arguing that character issues can be highly relevant to presidential performance. Yet students of American politics can examine the scholarship of such influential political scientists as Richard Neustadt, James David Barber, and George C. Edwards III in vain for suitable analytical tools to evaluate Lieberman's claim. Ironically, it may have taken the Clinton scandal to highlight the limitations of leading contemporary theories of presidential behavior and point out the need for a more comprehensive approach that includes an investigation of the relationship between personal virtue and presidential power and the ethical purposes that presidential power should serve.

The works of Neustadt, Barber, and Edwards typify major directions that research on the presidency has taken in recent decades. Neustadt's *Presidential Power*, originally published in 1960, arguably remains "the most important and influential expression" (Bessette and Tulis 1981, 4) of the kind of political analysis that goes beyond formal rules governing the executive branch to concentrate on how presidents actually behave. Barber's *Presidential Character*, written in 1972, helped to stimulate interest in and generate support for the emerging field of political psychology by successfully predicting how Richard Nixon and several of his successors would perform in the White House. The numerous quantitative studies of the presidency that Edwards has advanced over the past twenty-five years are noteworthy products of the post–World War II behavioral revolution in political science.

According to Richard Neustadt, presidential power in the United States is inhibited by a constitutional system that decentralizes and fragments government through the principles of checks and balances, separation of powers, and federalism. In order to exert influence under these circumstances, Neustadt argues, presidents must learn how to persuade others, who respond to different constituencies and are essentially immune to presidential fiat, that they share corresponding interests. Neustadt's celebrated scholarship thus serves as a training manual to teach presidents the skills of political persuasion, including which bargaining devices, or "vantage points" as he calls them (Neustadt 1990, 31), to use at each stage of the bargaining process in order to ensure maximum effectiveness. For presidents to ignore the function of persuasion in American politics, he concludes, is to risk being relegated to the role of something resembling a dignified clerk (1990, 7).

But what should presidents persuade others to do and what ethical standards should govern their behavior once they are in office? On the subject of the normative purposes of political power, Neustadt is silent. Since he chooses to tell us virtually nothing about the role of morality in politics, we are led to believe that presidential leadership involves little more than the arts of manipulation, cleverness, and cunning. According to political scientists Thomas Cronin and Michael Genovese, "many readers would have liked" Neustadt to provide "a more thoughtful discussion of the ends of presidential power, of the ethical boundaries," and address such questions as "what are the higher claims on a president and how does the creative president join together the ethic of responsibility and the ethic of ultimate ends?" (Cronin and Genovese 1998, 115).

Neustadt claims to be puzzled by these criticisms (Neustadt 1990, xvi). He recounts in amazement the story of being personally told by certain figures in the Nixon administration, who were implicated in the Watergate scandal, that *Presidential Power* served as a guide for their criminal activities. Conveniently ignoring the cutthroat quality that frequently marked Nixon's politics since the time he first ran for Congress in 1945, Neustadt argues that, if members of his White House staff had been more experienced in governmental relations and commanded a greater knowledge of American history, they would have been able to more fully appreciate the implied normative parameters of Neustadt's research and could have convinced Nixon not to violate them.

James David Barber's theories are also vulnerable to the charge of neglecting the connection between ideals and politics. Barber takes the position that the most effective way to evaluate presidential leadership is through the identification of psychological traits that are acquired at an early age and remain constant throughout a person's life, not issue orientations that tend to fluctuate from time to time. To aid in the evaluation process, he develops a four-celled typology of presidential personality that relies upon such factors as character, worldview, and style to help him measure how confidently aggressive presidents act and how much pleasure they derive from politics. On this basis he concludes that accomplished presidents will most likely be active-positive types who are "energetic, optimistic" politicians with a "flexibility in style and a world view containing a variety of probabilities (that) are congruent with a character ready for trial and error" (Barber 1992, 490). At the same time Barber warns us about active-negative chief executives whose feelings of inferiority, moodiness, and compulsive behavior frequently lead them to take intractable stands on political issues.

Like Neustadt, however, Barber does not address the ethical directions that aggressive presidents who enjoy their job should follow. When we speak of a person with character, we ordinarily mean someone who possesses integrity and moral strength. But Barber's definition of character is indifferent to such normative qualities. This critical omission may help to explain why a melancholic, self-doubting, and highly principled person such as Abraham Lincoln more closely fits the description of an active-negative president whom Barber predicts will turn out so badly. As political scientist Jeffrey Tulis suggests, if Lincoln had not vigorously pursued "the objectives he considered to be 'right,' " an attribute Barber regards as potentially detrimental to effective political leadership in the United States, it would have been impossible to preserve the Union during the Civil War (Tulis 1981, 301).

To political scientist Douglas Hoekstra, therefore,

> the analyses of both Neustadt and Barber have reductive tendencies, and it is primarily presidential intention or principle which is reduced to the terms of explanation offered by either power strategies or character. Both of these aspects of the presidency are obviously crucial, but may be most relevant to retrospective understandings of our most ordinary presidents. Claims of presidential greatness seem to rest on more than political skills or presidential character. (Hoekstra 1989, 286)

Along with Neustadt and Barber, George C. Edwards III is one of the foremost scholars seeking to gain knowledge of presidential behavior. Because, in his estimation, political scientists who study the office have not utilized statistical methods as rigorously and as objectively as possible, Edwards finds that in general they deserve to be held in "low regard" by their peers. "Research on the presidency, taken as a whole, has not advanced our understanding of the institution very far," he writes.

> Although we have innumerable descriptions of it and its occupants, we have a fundamental lack of understanding of why things happen as they do. We have generally not focused on explanations, that is, the relationships between two or more variables. Instead, we have usually examined only one side of the equation. This presents a striking paradox: the single most important institution in American politics is the one that political scientists understand the least. (Edwards 1983, 99–100)

Of course, by Edwards's own admission, evaluating the inherent fairness of competing presidential policies and the moral posture that presidents exhibit in office is logically inconsistent with the goal of scientific objectivity. For example, one of Edwards's statistical studies investigates the relationship between the popularity of presidents and their political power. Even presidents with high public approval ratings, he argues in *Presidential Influence in Congress*, cannot be certain that Congress will pass their legislative programs (Edwards 1980, 100). However, Edwards's statistics are unable to explain whether the substance of a president's legislative program actually merits public approval and congressional support. These concerns involve value judgments that are beyond the competence of objective analysis.

This inconsistency is also illustrated in the 1999 edition of *Presidential Leadership*, a text Edwards coauthored with political scientist Stephen Wayne. In Appendix A of their text, Edwards and Wayne observe that "normative questions and arguments have always occupied a substantial percentage of the presidential literature, and rightly so" (Edwards and Wayne 1999, 511). Yet the authors also note that scholars who use traditional methods to study the presidency generally reach normative conclusions that are "subjective, fragmentary and impressionistic" (508). In their Prologue, moreover, Edwards and Wayne raise the question of whether Bill Clinton, "who has been found to be engaging in immoral behavior in the Oval Office," can continue to provide the moral leadership required of effective presidents (xx). Yet one wonders why the authors do not consider their own normative analysis of Clinton's leadership capabilities to be equally "subjective, fragmentary and impressionistic."

In view of its missing normative component, Hoekstra concludes that the contemporary study of the presidency

> cannot fully understand its subject within the domains currently defined by some of its leading practitioners, with their tendency to abstract out single clusters of variables, whether centered on power-seeking or the resources of personality. Joining these important concerns to a recognition of the historical and normative dimensions of the presidency would seem to require a more synoptic approach, or the renewal of an older conception of social science, in which the boundaries between social science, history and philosophy become more permeable. (Hoekstra 1989, 296)

Now the synoptic approach that Hoekstra admires, and finds misplaced in contemporary presidential scholarship, was originally developed by Aristotle. Aristotle's methodology for studying political leadership does not preclude consideration of the factors that analysts such as Neustadt, Barber, and Edwards emphasize. Aristotle's leaders are thus persuasive, energetic persons who take pride in their work and would not be above utilizing cutting-edge technology and sophisticated statistical methods to gauge the opinions of their constituents. But they are leaders, not followers, and their behavior is consciously governed by explicit moral standards that are accessible to reasonable men and women everywhere.

There can be no doubt that Neustadt, Barber, and Edwards's analytical tools are bona fide methods for studying certain aspects of presidential politics. But their methods either obfuscate or preclude consideration of the normative issues that interest Aristotle and that also constitute a critical aspect of political leadership. As such, they represent incomplete methodologies that are incapable of adequately explaining the political relevance of Bill Clinton's recent unseemly conduct in the White House.

It is the thesis of *The Prudential Presidency*, indeed, that the model of political leadership based on the concept of prudence that Aristotle introduced 2,300 years ago remains the most realistic approach available to this day for understanding the qualities necessary for presidents to succeed in office. As the following chapters attempt to demonstrate, presidents serve the public interest of the United States most effectively when their behavior conforms to Aristotle's venerable, but no longer generally venerated, theory of political prudence.

Chapter 2 discusses Aristotle's theory of prudence and explains the differences between prudence and the competing leadership strategies that his theory implies—idealism, cynicism, and pragmatism. Aristotelian prudence has been described as "the virtue of reason in its practical employment" (Dahl 1984, 107). Political scientist Erwin Hargrove defines it as the rare capacity to "keep in mind not only the absolute best, but the best in the historical context" (Hargrove 1998, 7). Essentially, prudent political leaders are able to translate morally preferable ideals into politically feasible policies. They possess the remarkable ability to reconcile morality with practical politics without compromising the integrity of their ideals. In contrast, idealists and cynics repudiate practical politics and morality altogether. Pragmatists like to talk about ideals but are more willing than prudent leaders to bargain them away for the sake of political power.

Succeeding chapters develop the relationship of one of the four competing leadership strategies to presidential decisions, behavior, and policies that appear to most clearly illustrate its meaning and significance. Analysis of the clearest illustration comes first. Others follow chronologically. Chapter 3 examines the prudential quality of such successful policies as Abraham Lincoln's position on slavery and conduct of the Civil War, George Washington's attitude toward the founding of the United States, Theodore Roosevelt's conservationism, and Franklin Delano Roosevelt's management of our participation in World War II. Chapter 4 explores the relationship between idealism and the critical mistakes that led to Woodrow Wilson's inability to convince the United States Senate to ratify the Treaty of Versailles, John Quincy Adams's misunderstanding of patronage, Jimmy Carter's Mariel boat lift fiasco, and the defeat of Bill Clinton's health care initiative.

Chapter 5 describes the cynicism that defines the involvements of Richard Nixon with Watergate, Thomas Jefferson with the Aaron Burr trial for treason, Franklin Delano Roosevelt with internment of Japanese Americans during World War II, and Bill Clinton with lying about adultery in the Oval Office. Chapter 6 investigates the pragmatism underlying the responses of Harry Truman to the proposal to drop the atomic bomb on Japan, Dwight Eisenhower to McCarthyism, John Kennedy to the Bay of Pigs invasion, and Bill Clinton to the issue of gays in the military.

A conscious effort has been made to avoid evaluating presidents themselves. It is necessary to emphasize this distinction between presidents and the policies they support because American chief executives are complex human beings who have not remained consistently prudent, idealistic, cynical, or pragmatic throughout their careers. Even Abraham Lincoln, who arguably fulfilled the standards of Aristotelian leadership more closely than any other president, sometimes veered off course. In 1862 he supported a plan to deport slaves liberated by the Civil War to Central America—a cynical attempt made by White Americans to shirk responsibility for those they had brought over to the United States in chains. At the other end of the spectrum, the frequently cynical Richard Nixon took the prudent step in 1972 of reestablishing diplomatic relations with the People's Republic of China.

This volume defends the proposition that Aristotelian prudence represents the quality most conducive to effective presidential behavior. It does not claim that all presidents who behave prudentially make a conscious effort to abide by Aristotle's theory of political leadership. The overwhelming majority of them probably never heard of it. "Prudence" simply is the word Aristotle used to describe what leaders do when they are able to serve the public interest. Neither is it being claimed that presidents who attempt to serve the public interest are assured of success, whether they consciously abide by Aristotle or not. Prudence is a process that depends upon the fortuitous confluence of a leader's often fragile inner resources with political, economic, and social conditions that frequently are beyond the leader's control.

Nor does every presidential decision fit neatly into one of Aristotle's categories. Why did George Washington send 13,000 soldiers in 1794 to suppress the so-called Whiskey Rebellion of a small number of farmers in western Pennsylvania? Was his goal to prudently establish the legal authority of the American government on the U.S. frontier? Or was he trying to cynically usurp executive authority? What possessed Theodore Roosevelt to abruptly announce at the beginning of his first full term that he would not run for reelection in 1908? And what convinced him to change his mind in 1912, split the Republican party, and cause Woodrow Wilson to emerge victorious? Was his initial decision an idealistic effort to defend the American tradition of presidents serving only two terms? Was his change of mind a pragmatic ploy to replace William Howard Taft in office or a cynical attempt to regain power for himself?

Why were 47,000 American troops lost on the battlefields of Vietnam? Did they die in an idealistic effort by presidents to save a third world nation from totalitarian oppression? Or were their deaths part of a cynical interference with a weaker nation's internal affairs in order to preserve and expand American interests in Southeast Asia? What led Ronald Reagan to precipitate the Iran-Contra scandal of 1987? Was he acting in an idealistic fashion to free innocent American hostages held in Iran, pragmatically in retaliation against Communist aggression in Latin America, or cynically to evade congressional limits on American involvement in Nicaragua? Washington's reaction to the Whiskey Rebellion, Theodore Roosevelt's hasty decision not to seek reelection, American participation in the Vietnam War, and Reagan's connection to the Iran-Contra scandal represent prime examples of erroneous presidential decisions caused by confused objectives, aims, and goals. Since the errors committed in such instances are so convoluted, it does not make sense to affix an intellectual label to them.

By the same token the theories of prudence, idealism, cynicism, and pragmatism are unable to completely account for presidential incompetence. For example, the problems facing the Union when James Buchanan became president in 1857 were so grave that even the most prudent leader would have been frustrated by them. Unfortunately, Buchanan allowed the gravity of the occasion to overwhelm him. The message he sent to Congress on December 3, 1860, in the face of South Carolina's secession read "like a confession of weakness on the part of a discredited Executive as he neared the end of a disastrous term" (Malone and Rauch 1960c, 154). "The slavery question, like everything human, will have its day," Buchanan duly noted on that date. "I firmly believe that it has reached and passed the culminating point. But if in the midst of the existing excitement the Union shall perish, the evil may then be irreparable" (Buchanan quoted in Hirschfield 1982, 72).

Moreover, it is clear that Warren G. Harding was not directly implicated in the corrupt practices of his secretary of the interior, Albert Fall, that led to the infamous 1921 "Teapot Dome affair." Fall convinced Harding to switch jurisdiction over naval oil reserves in California and Wyoming to his department and then proceeded to lease the reserves to private oil companies in exchange for bribes worth hundreds of thousands of dollars. Nevertheless, it also is clear that Harding's inept appointments, radical delegation of presidential authority to crooked subordinates, and lax moral standards created a sleazy atmosphere in the White House that made the scandal possible. For the most part incompetence, not imprudence, was Buchanan's and Harding's major failing in these instances.

What roles do intention and consequence play in the definition of prudent political leadership? On the one hand, actions cannot be deemed prudent if they do not result in consequences that successfully serve the public interest. Good intentions simply are insufficient. On the other hand, successful consequences do not themselves meet the standards of prudence. Leaders can only be defined as prudent when they intend for a certain policy to succeed and then are fortunate enough to achieve their desired results. For example, the defeat of Franklin Delano Roosevelt's infamous Supreme Court–packing scheme of 1937, discussed at greater length in chapter 7, may have had the positive result for the United States of humbling him and moderating his tendency for presidential hubris and imperiousness. Since FDR did not expect to be humbled by it, however, the scheme cannot be accurately characterized as prudent.

While Aristotle's theory of prudence does provide a methodology that can be utilized to evaluate presidential decision making in general, it does not come equipped with a crystal ball that determines exactly what decisions presidents should make at any given time. The very best that can be done in this regard is to evaluate specific policy choices by the fundamental values and perspectives that his theory employs. That is the general approach I have tried to take in subsequent chapters. Readers undoubtedly will object to some of my specific policy evaluations. But they should not permit these objections to close their minds to the possibility that Aristotle's basic methodology bears a crucial relevance for contemporary presidential scholarship.

Is it really fair to play "Monday morning quarterback" and hold presidents responsible for what, only later, prove to be mistaken decisions? Aren't there too many "what ifs" involved in this equation? In 1807 war between the United States and Britain was imminent. That year the British frigate *Leopold*, searching for deserters, seized an American ship off the port of Norfolk, Virginia. President Jefferson decided to retaliate, not through armed conflict as many Americans would have preferred, but by employing economic sanctions against Great Britain and the other European countries engaged in the Napoleonic Wars of the time. The resulting Embargo Act, passed by Congress at Jefferson's request, essentially put an end to American trade. Severe and lasting damage to the economy of the United States was only averted by its repeal in 1809.

The embargo turned out to be one of the worst policies associated with the Jefferson administration. "To this day," political scientist Leonard Levy argues, "it remains the most repressive and unconstitutional legislation ever enacted by Congress in time of peace" (Levy 1963, 139). Can Jefferson be blamed for the disastrous effects of the embargo? Isn't it always better to avoid war? How could he have predicted what would happen? Clearly these are are not easy questions to answer. Yet the fact remains that vision is precisely the quality that confers distinction upon Aristotelian prudence and makes it the outstanding form of political leadership. By definition, a prudent policy is one that is capable of seeing the present in the context of the past and future. In this instance, however, Jefferson displayed "myopia," not vision, and damaged both his own reputation and the public interest of the United States (McDonald 1994, 273).

Can presidents sometimes be trapped by events that severely limit their freedom to choose between alternative courses of action? Of course they can. But prudent leaders possess extraordinary inner resources and political talents that are lacking in idealists, cynics, and pragmatists, and that facilitate freedom of choice. Their moral imagination allows them to envision the public interest of a given polity. Their foresight permits them to spy potential snags in the culture and obstacles in the political system that could impede the realization of the public interest. Their experience in government teaches them about the techniques that can be used to steer clear of the snags and overcome many of the obstacles. And their ingenuity allows them to put those techniques to practical use.

Consider John F. Kennedy and the plan for invading Cuba that he inherited from the outgoing administration of Dwight D. Eisenhower. The reasons why Kennedy decided to launch the invasion at the Bay of Pigs in 1961 are developed in chapter 6. Suffice it to say that Kennedy went against what he later claimed to be his better judgment because he did not feel he had the political clout at the beginning of his own administration to successfully challenge such influential supporters of the plan as the U.S. State Department, the Central Intelligence Agency, and Cuban-American interest groups.

Yet the evidence indicates that there may have been another motive behind Kennedy's decision. Throughout his career in Congress, including his refusal to support the United States Senate's censure of the Red-baiting demagogue Joseph McCarthy in 1954 (see chapter 6), his 1960 campaign for the presidency that urged Americans to shrink the supposed "missile gap" with the Soviet Union, his backing of political coups in South Vietnam, and his precipitation of the Cuban Missile crisis in 1962, Kennedy demonstrated that he appeared to share the narrow cold war mentality that then dominated the formulation of American foreign policy. Considered from this perspective, it can be concluded that Kennedy became entrapped at the Bay of Pigs mainly by his own imprudent views, not just by events over which he claimed to have had little or no control in 1961.

Herein lies one of the most compelling features of Aristotelian prudence. In its attempt to envision practical means by which to reconcile immaterial ideals with material circumstances, prudence may lead to the discovery of new, more realistic directions that a nation's policies may take. Had Kennedy provided prudent leadership in 1961, he could have recognized the futility of the cold war mentality and tried his best to steer American public opinion away from that mentality and the invasion of Cuba it spawned. He could have predicted that the stockpiling of nuclear warheads occurring during the cold war would continue to threaten our existence long after the cold war ended. Certainly the level of political prescience required for presidents to provide such a high level of leadership has ever been rare. For precisely the reason that prudence is easier said than done, Aristotle presented it, not as a panacea for ineffectual politics, but as a paradigm that beckons leaders to serve the public interest as best as they possibly can.

If Aristotle is unable to provide a comprehensive description of every president and every presidential decision, and if Aristotle's strategy of prudent leadership cannot provide presidents with a precise, step-by-step formula for success, why should we be interested in returning to his theories? Chapter 7 reveals the unique ethical dimension that Aristotle contributes to an analysis of the American presidency. What he offers us, in short, is an emphasis on morality that avoids both naivete and moralism and a theory of prudence that neglects neither ideals nor the sometimes nasty business of politics that make it possible for ethics to influence public policy. There is little room for pretense or illusion in a process that simultaneously facilitates the ennoblement of politics by ideals and the contamination of ideals by politics. This concluding chapter also attempts to explain why contemporary students of presidential leadership have often neglected Aristotle's contribution and seeks to identify the consequences of their neglect.

It is one thing to write about political leadership in general; but it is another to discuss the specific dilemmas confronting chief executives in the United States. In the nineteenth century such eminent foreign observers of American democracy as Alexis de Tocqueville and James Bryce noted its governing paradox: while notoriously independent, Americans appear to require energetic leadership perhaps more than other people; the American principles of equality and individualism seem to preclude the possibility of energetic leadership by implying that no human being possesses the right to tell another what to do.

In the second half of the twentieth century Richard Neustadt developed Tocqueville's and Bryce's idea by explaining how our historic distrust of centralized government, reflected in the American pluralist system that establishes no definite constitutional locus of political authority, makes the struggle by presidents to exercise power a particularly arduous one. More recently Jeffrey Tulis has pointed out that when modern presidents have attempted to evade these formidable cultural and legal obstacles to their power by constructing a "rhetorical presidency," the quality of American politics has tended to deteriorate in the process. According to Tulis, the direct appeal to voters by modern presidents often has contributed to the decline of public discourse and the creation of simplistic, short-term solutions to complex policy questions (Tulis 1987, 202).

What manner of men and women are prudent leaders? What character traits predispose them to act so realistically? Lincoln's basic attitude toward slavery and overall direction of the Civil War demonstrate that leadership constitutes a deeply elusive, mysterious phenomenon that confounds scholarly attempts to fully understand it through the use of standard contemporary psychological profiles of successful presidents. "The biographer cannot be satisfied with labelling his subject as being an instance of, or bearing a certain resemblance to, a pure type," political scientist Alexander George claims.

> To do so oversimplifies the task of making use of theories and findings of dynamic psychology and personality studies, and is likely to yield results of a limited and disappointing character. . . . *Classification is often confused with diagnosis.* To tag the subject with a label drawn from a typology, to place him in a pigeonhole of one of its pure types, does not provide what the biographer needs most: namely, a more discriminating, differentiated theory regarding the individual's more complex personality. (George 1974, 273. All italics in this book are the authors' own.)

In this book I have tried to avoid the fallacies of pigeonholing and stereotyping by portraying the leadership strategies of prudence, idealism, cynicism, and pragmatism as paradigms that pertain only to certain presidential decisions reached by certain presidents at certain times during their presidencies. My analysis intentionally does not claim the relevance of Aristotelian typologies for every decision made by individual presidents while they occupied the Oval Office.

It may be possible to make some very general observations about the personality of prudent leaders, however. According to Aristotle, they are highly principled, forceful people whose hard-boiled will, strength of character, and breadth of knowledge about the future consequences of present actions prevent their dedication to personal as well as social justice from devolving into either blind idealism, amoral cynicism, or lukewarm pragmatism. To Aristotle, moreover, these traits are inborn and developed over a lifetime of political experience. The eminent theologian Reinhold Niebuhr further describes prudent leaders as hardy souls who have the potential to soar "beyond the possibilities of history" as well as to adapt to specific historical contexts. They are able to accept responsibility for realizing "their individual ideals in their common life," Niebuhr argues, while simultaneously reaching the ineluctable conclusion that "society remains man's great fulfillment and his great frustration" (Niebuhr 1932, 82).

In order to minimize misunderstanding, let me explain at the outset what *The Prudential Presidency* seeks to accomplish. It does not include a comprehensive review of literature on the presidency and Aristotle's thought. Nor does it not purport to offer scholars finely nuanced case studies based upon new data about presidential politics. It attempts rather to provide a straightforward application of an ancient strategy for effective leadership to information presently available in a language and style accessible to general readers and students in courses on the American presidency and the history of political philosophy. I would like to think that my applications are at least somewhat original and that their inventiveness will perform the heuristic function of inspiring my intended audience to learn more about Aristotle and the office of the president. For example, I am not aware of other studies that explicitly compare Aristotelian prudence to idealism, cynicism, and pragmatism. Nevertheless, it never occurred to me that the book would be capable of establishing a major intellectual breakthrough in the treatment of these subjects.

With this book, in effect, I am attempting to offer readers an exercise in what used to be called civic education. Toward that end, I consciously chose breadth over depth in calculating the number of presidential decisions and policies to examine according to the standards of Aristotelian prudence. Many of the students I teach unfortunately lack basic knowledge of American history and government. They are products of the widespread cultural illiteracy in the United States about which scholars such as Allan Bloom and E. D. Hirsch have written (Bloom 1987; Hirsch 1987). Since students will constitute a major part of the book's readership, I felt that it would make more sense to provide them with a greater range of information by discussing a wider variety of issues—even if a degree of subtlety had to be sacrificed in the process.

By introducing students both to the dynamics of presidential decision-making and to Aristotelian logic, *The Prudential Presidency* also seeks to demonstrate the value of interdisciplinary studies. Its purpose is to convince readers that presidential research does not have to lack explicit philosophical content and that philosophy can go beyond abstractions to furnish a practical standard to rate the styles of governance and personal behavior of presidential candidates and presidents alike. All scholarship is based on certain assumptions about reality and human nature that, in most cases, are unconsciously held. I am merely asking that these unstated assumptions be brought out into the open, where they can undergo the rational reflection that is supposed to be the hallmark of the academic community, and be applied to events that are covered in history books and featured on the evening news.

While this book is occasioned by the events and controversies surrounding the recent Clinton-Lewinsky scandal, its genesis goes back much further. It is based on a course on the American presidency that I have been teaching at a number of colleges and universities for over thirty years. Since I have never been able to find texts that accurately and effectively reflect my interdisciplinary approach to the course, I finally decided to write one of my own. There has been much talk but little action in the academic community about the value of building intellectual bridges across subject areas. *The Prudential Presidency* represents a modest effort to achieve that goal.

Many presidential scholars tend to reject out of hand Aristotle and the accumulated wisdom of the Western political tradition for being deficient in the technical sophistication required by their research. Students need to be reminded that such a tradition exists and that it contains profound knowledge about the nature of political leadership. They also must be put on guard against the risk of trivializing politics by abandoning the traditional moral vision of the West in favor of a strictly incremental approach. Since our "own private stock of reason . . . is small," Edmund Burke writes, "individuals would do better to avail themselves of the general bank and capital of nations and ages" (Burke 1955, 99). "When we stand upon the shoulders of those who have gone before us," political scientist John Hallowell observes, paraphrasing Burke, "we increase our vision. . . . The newest is not necessarily the best nor the latest necessarily the truest" (Hallowell 1950, 195–96).

Many political philosophers are content to detach themselves from pressing issues of the day by concentrating exclusively on close textual exegeses of the great texts that constitute the Western political tradition. Students need to be made aware that, while profiting from the Western tradition admittedly is not possible unless accurate exegeses are available, an exclusive reliance on textual scrutiny can lead to the impression that political philosophy is an "effete but pretentious activity" and may produce what political scientist John Gunnell has called the alienation of political philosophy from politics (Gunnell 1986, ix). Along with splitting hairs over what Aristotle means by prudence in a certain sentence on a certain page in one of his works, therefore, students must encourage political philosophers to "create a usable past" (Levy 1988, 30) by explaining how Aristotle's concept can provide insights into the specific dilemmas faced by contemporary leaders. The great Western thinkers considered their ideas to be pertinent for all times, places, and issues. Contemporary disciples of these great thinkers must be reminded by their students to reemphasize their pertinence.

Aristotle's most basic legacy to us is warnings about overspecialization in education and reductionism in politics. His intellectual ideal is *paideia*, the erudition associated with broadly based learning. Narrowly trained specialists, he argues, cannot possibly appreciate the complex interrelationship of ideas and behavior that defines every aspect of human existence. By the same token, the prudent leaders Aristotle celebrates cannot be reduced to the level of a one-dimensional stereotype. They are not liberal, conservative, socialist, or capitalist and conform to none of the psychological labels with which we are familiar. Their goal instead is to do the very best they can under the circumstances as realistically and with as much justice and decency as possible. Toward that end they strive to reconcile what many people today would consider to be irreconcilable: abstract ideals with concrete situations, rights with responsibilities, the present with the past and future, theory with practice, facts with values, and humankind's propensity for evil with our potential for good.

By taking an interdisciplinary approach to the study of the American chief executive and by offering prudence as an alternative to reductionist analyses of presidential politics in the United States, *The Prudential Presidency* seeks to reaffirm Aristotle's legacy. Now that the office of the presidency is in crisis over the issue of moral leadership, perhaps the time is right to return to his political philosophy and give a renewed hearing to the views he and his intellectual heirs in the history of Western thought ask us to consider.

CHAPTER 2

Aristotelian Prudence

In the third century B.C. Aristotle studied the leadership traits of history's most successful rulers and discovered that their success was based primarily on the exercise of *phronesis* or prudence, the term he coined to represent a leader's ability to "calculate well for the attainment of a particular end of a fine sort" (Aristotle 1966, 176). The model for Aristotle's *phronimos* or prudent political ruler is Pericles, the great Athenian lawgiver. Pericles, Aristotle writes, possessed "the power of seeing what is good for (himself) and for humanity" (177).

Among the occasions that Pericles demonstrated the prudent quality of his leadership was during the Peloponnesian War in 429 B.C. when Athens was besieged by Sparta. Against the masses who panicked in the face of the siege, Pericles urged solidarity and caution. Against the majority who desired to counterattack against the full strength of the Spartan forces, Pericles proposed that they rely on their navy and concentrate on defense of the city. Against those Athenians who wished to use the war as a means to expand their empire, Pericles advised restraint. "For as long as he was at the head of state during the peace, he pursued a moderate and conservative policy; and in his time its greatness was at its height," the Greek historian Thucydides explains:

When the war broke out, here also he seems to have rightly gauged the power of his country. . . . He told them to wait quietly, to pay attention to their marine, to attempt no new conquests, and to expose the city to no hazards during the war, and doing this, promised them a favorable result. . . . Pericles, indeed, by his rank, ability, and known integrity, was enabled to exercise an independent control over the multitude—in short, to lead them instead of being led by them; for as he never sought power by improper means, he was never compelled to flatter them, but, on the contrary, enjoyed so high an estimation that he could afford to anger them by contradiction. When he saw them unseasonably and insolently elated, he would with a word reduce them to alarm; on the other hand, if they fell victims to a panic, he could at once restore them to confidence. (Thucydides 1951, 120)

Aristotle observes that political leaders such as Pericles retain distinctive talents that permit them to convert ideals into practical policy. According to Aristotle, these talents include the desire to serve the public interest of a society by treating all of its citizens with fairness and justice; the capacity to define a society's public interest by envisioning its present needs in light of its past successes and failures and future hopes and fears; the talent to create laws and policies that accurately reflect their vision and successfully meet the needs of citizens; and the skill to convince others to obey the laws.

At the heart of Aristotle's theory of prudent leadership lie certain assumptions about reality and human nature. Aristotle assumes that reality consists primarily of transcendent immaterial ideals and, to a lesser extent, of transitory material representations of these ideals. To Aristotle, for example, the reality of a square is based on a perfect universal definition imperfectly realized in material squares that are never completely true.

Aristotle also believes that human beings are qualitatively different from all other living things because, in addition to our bodies, we have souls that give us the power to comprehend transcendence and choose between right and wrong. "It is the peculiarity of man, in comparison with the rest of the animal world," Aristotle writes, "that he alone possesses a perception of good and evil, of the just and unjust, and of other similar qualities" (Aristotle 1962, 6). For Aristotle, therefore, human existence represents a dramatic struggle between our immortal souls that inspire us to achieve supreme happiness throughout time by loving our neighbors as ourselves, and our bodily instincts that conspire to convince us to settle for instant gratification by loving ourselves alone.

Since Aristotle realizes that humans alone can make moral choices, he is not at all shocked when we choose to make immoral ones. His view of human nature, in other words, takes seriously both our capacity for justice and potential for evil. Reinhold Niebuhr neatly captures that view when he locates the human condition as "standing in the paradoxical situation of freedom and finiteness" (Niebuhr 1941, 192). Like Niebuhr, Aristotle believes each time we congratulate ourselves for a job well done and come to the conclusion that we are essentially good, we fall prey to the sin of pride. Each time we question our intentions and consider ourselves to be essentially evil, our ability to reach such a judgment "would seem to negate (its) context" (2).

Indeed, it is because Aristotle entertains no illusions about the ability of the flesh to undermine even the most basic standards of decency that he stresses the importance of ideals in his views of reality and human nature and his theory of prudence. As imperfect creatures, he teaches, we must strive for moral perfection through rational control of our animal passions if we want to gain some measure of justice and fulfillment in our lives. "Rather ought we," he writes, "so far as in us lies, to put on immortality and to live in conformity with the highest thing within us" (Aristotle 1966, 305).

Consistent with his views of reality and human nature Aristotle develops a definition of political justice that relies upon a balance between individual rights, "doing what one likes" (Aristotle 1962, 234), and moral responsibility, choosing to follow the univeral laws of common decency. On the one hand, Aristotle maintains, citizens must be permitted to enjoy enough autonomy to exercise the gift of free will that makes us human. At the same time, citizens must be held accountable for the effects their freely willed choices have on others. When citizens are denied sufficient autonomy, he concludes, a society is created that is inhospitable to human beings. When freedom outweighs responsibility, political justice breaks down and is replaced by what Aristotle describes as "licentiousness" (233).

Aristotle develops the rationale for his theory of prudence in Book VI of his *Nicomachean Ethics*. There he distinguishes between the theoretical and practical forms of reason and the intellectual and moral virtues or talents that each form of reason employs. Theoretical reason and the intellectual talents, he argues, apply to such subjects as metaphysics and mathematics that are learned in abstract for their own sake and yield universal truths that cannot be affected by human volition. Practical reason and the moral talents, on the other hand, apply to subjects such as ethics and politics that yield truths that hold true in but a majority of cases and involve knowledge of the noblest human motives for the sake of noble action. The task of practical reason and the moral talents, according to Aristotle, is to take the first principles discovered by the intellect and integrate them with life experiences.

For example, it would be imprudent to select professors of human anatomy and human physiology to operate on sick people. Although professors possess theoretical knowledge of anatomy and physiology, they do not have the background and know-how necessary to make split-second, life-saving decisions based upon anatomical abnormalities. Everyone's gall bladder is not located in precisely the same place, after all. As a rule, therefore, operations should be performed by surgeons, who apply knowledge they learn from professors to the practice of medicine (Hallowell and Porter 1997, 68).

Aristotle compares the prudence of Pericles to the theoretical reason of Thales and Anaxagoras, two contemporaries whom he depicts as "exceptional" and "deep" thinkers. While admitting that Thales and Anaxagoras "are no doubt wise," Aristotle argues that they "lack common sense" and that their thought "is useless" for politics because "it is not the good of humanity that they explore." Since, to Aristotle, prudence "does concern itself with human affairs," he describes it as the architectonic talent that precedes and overarches all others (Aristotle 1966, 180). As philosopher Ronald Beiner explains:

> *Phronesis* is not one virtue among others, but is the master virtue that encompasses and orders the various individual virtues. Virtue is the exercise of ethical knowledge as elicited by particular situations of action, and to act on the basis of this knowledge as a matter of course is to possess *phronesis*. Without *phronesis* one cannot properly be said to possess *any* of the virtues, and to possess *phronesis* is, conversely, to possess *all* the virtues, for *phronesis* is knowledge of which virtue is appropriate in particular circumstances, and the ability to act on that knowledge. *Phronesis* is a comprehensive moral capacity because it involves seeing particular situations in their true light in interaction with a general grasp of what it is to be a complete human being, and to live a proper human life. (Beiner 1983, 73)

According to Aristotle, the unique value of prudence for politics is its ability to explain how to realize abstract ends through the concrete means available to human beings so that we may do the right thing to the right person at the right time "for the right motive and in the right way" (Aristotle 1966, 65). In order to meet the standards of prudence, he argues, political leaders are required to do their very best to create policies that prevent the subversion of moral ideals even under the direst circumstances. Prudent leaders aim high but accept less when their efforts inevitably and invariably fall short of the mark. They never give up hope for a better world even as they respect the obstacles to such hope. They expect neither too little nor too much from the politics they practice.

But first things first. Before prudent leaders can decide how to reconcile material circumstances with universal ideals, they are obliged to determine what specific ideal should be applied to what specific situation. "Since, in practical life, there are always multiple ends to pursue [e.g., security and freedom, inclusiveness and excellence, etc.]," political scientist Richard Ruderman writes, "*phronesis* should determine, at any given time, which end to pursue [in light of the resources, not least the moral resources, required to pursue it]" (Ruderman 1997, 416). For Ruderman, therefore, "the beginning of prudence is the recognition that conflict [of principle as well as interest] is a permanent part of political life" (416).

This obligation of prudent leaders to do the best they can under the circumstances is illustrated by Aristotle's treatment of entrenched plutocratic and tyrannical governments in Book V of his *Politics*. He cannot justify rule by the rich because he realizes that governing well is not directly related to acquiring money. Tyranny represents the antithesis of political justice to him because it elevates the self-interest of the tyrant over the public good. The strategy he recommends that prudent leaders use to reform these regimes involves exploiting the greed that underlies them. According to Aristotle, the prudent leader should warn plutocrats and tyrants that their refusal to share power will result ultimately in their violent overthrow and death. Through his actions, Aristotle argues, the prudent leader does not expect to create virtuous rulers out of corrupt ones. Rather, recognizing that wholesale political change in the cases of entrenched plutocracies and tyrannies may be neither feasible, because the rulers control all of the sources of power, nor advisable, because the alternative may be worse than the status quo, he employs his energies to move the regimes closer, if only by millimeters, to the ideal of a just state.

Prudence may be contrasted to other strategies of political leadership such as idealism, cynicism and pragmatism. While proponents of prudence assume that reality is composed primarily of transcendent immaterial ideals, manifested in material phenomena, idealists believe that ideals alone constitute reality. Whereas proponents of prudence realize that humans routinely are seduced by powerful passions and can spoil even the best opportunities, idealists have a very high opinion of what people can accomplish and do not fear doing the theoretically right thing, right here and right now regardless of practical consequences. Reinhold Niebuhr calls idealists "the children of light" and describes them as foolish because they underestimate "the power of self-will" among human beings, including themselves (Niebuhr 1944, 11). Idealistic political leaders thus would excoriate Aristotle's plutocrats and tyrants, and foment rebellion. In the end, they would be murdered and their followers subjected to even greater injustices by a paranoid regime.

Cynics take a very different approach to politics. They do not believe in universal ideals, deny that qualitative differences exist between human beings and other living things, and are remorselessly selfish. Niebuhr terms cynics "the children of darkness" and depicts them as evil because they "know no law beyond their will and interest" (9). Consequently, cynical leaders initially would fawn on the plutocrats and tyrants by providing counsel on how they could further consolidate their control. Having firmly established themselves in the rulers' good graces, they might later advise them to initiate a policy of "bread and circuses," which they would arrange to administer, thereby gaining sufficient power among the poor and disenfranchised to frighten the rulers into sharing control with them.

Pragmatists reverse the relationship between universal ideals and material circumstances found in Aristotle's theory of prudence. They stress moral principles less than idealists and proponents of prudence but more than cynics. They have a lower opinion of human nature than idealists but a higher one than cynics. They are more optimistic than proponents of prudence as well because of their conviction that human beings can get along quite well most of the time without the support of enduring ethical guidelines. Pragmatic political leaders are thus less apprehensive than proponents of prudence about the lasting results of seeking immediate palpable benefits through effective use of the means at hand. Rather than warn the plutocrats and tyrants of the inevitable consequences of injustice, they might seek to persuade them to undertake certain civic improvements as monuments to their rule, thereby promoting the public interest while ensuring their own favor among the powerful.

Unlike their counterparts, prudent leaders seek to apply to politics the same tension between the intangible and tangible that they perceive in the universe. Prudent political leaders thus stress the immutable and the transcendent, but not to the exclusion of the imminent and the transitory. They accent forever but still pay close attention to today. They look first to the universal but are not blind to particulars. They stress the forest but do not neglect the trees. They view human behavior with a compassion that does not preclude toughness. They are not prepared to justify human pettiness even as they understand its underlying source.

It comes down to a question of priorities. If political leaders deal only with ethical values, they are idealists. If political leaders mock values, they are cynics. If, in their deliberations, values are secondary to tangible results, they are pragmatists. And if they emphasize universal ideals without romanticizing them and do their best to honor values in the face of practical obstacles, they are prudent leaders in the Aristotelian sense.

Because prudent political leaders emphasize moral principles, cynics and pragmatists often accuse them of being idealists. Because prudent leaders struggle to balance fixed moral principles with diverse issues, idealists often accuse them of being cynics or pragmatists. But neither of these accusations is accurate. Although prudent leaders reconcile immaterial ideals with material circumstances, they do not undermine ideals. Instead they seek to raise the ethical level of power politics. They facilitate justice by striving to secure proximate morality in an essentially immoral world. Nor do they entertain idealistic notions about what can be accomplished by politics in the name of justice.

Proponents of prudence, idealism, cynicism, and pragmatism react differently to the Judeo-Christian principle of "love thy neighbor as thyself." Within the context of this principle "thy neighbor" refers to every person who ever lived, is presently living, and will ever live. Since it is empirically impossible to love people we have never met in person, "thy neighbor" represents an abstract ideal. "Thyself" refers to material conditions, on the other hand, since the most tangible thing about us is our desire to fulfill our animal instincts, especially the instinct to survive. By definition idealists, who understand reality to be composed completely of ideals and have a very optimistic view of human nature, love their neighbors so much that they are more than willing to sacrifice their own lives for them.

Cynics, who understand reality to be composed completely of material things and have a very low opinion of human nature, love themselves alone and care nothing about their neighbors. As explained earlier, pragmatists, whose comprehension of reality emphasizes material things but does not ignore ideals, possess a relatively optimistic view of people because they are confident that human existence can be sustained without emphasizing ideals. For pragmatists, consequently, loving thyself takes precedence over loving thy neighbor. The awareness of reality for prudent leaders, however, stresses ideals over material circumstances. Their view of human nature is relatively pessimistic, moreover, since they do not believe that we can do much loving of people other than ourselves without leaning on ideals for support and encouragement. Prudent leaders thus are prepared to love their neighbors at least as much as they love themselves. They will risk their lives for their neighbors, in other words, but are extremely hesitant to do so.

In the thirteenth century St. Thomas Aquinas developed this line of thinking by shaping Aristotelian prudence into the first of Christianity's cardinal virtues. Next in rank in Aquinas's order are justice, fortitude, and virtue. He writes: "Omnis virtus moralis debet esse prudens" [all virtue is necessarily prudent]" (Aquinas quoted in Pieper 1959, 5). Like Aristotle, moreover, he argues that "it is necessary for the prudent man to know both the universal principles of reason and the singulars with which ethical action is concerned" (10). Aquinas thus advises prudent rulers not to pass laws and initiate policies that surpass the virtue of their citizens. He recommends instead that they design a political agenda according to the higher law standards of justice and then reconcile those standards with their citizens' demonstrated capacity to follow them. "Human law is framed for the mass of men, the majority of whom are not perfectly virtuous," Aquinas writes. "Therefore human law does not prohibit every vice from which virtuous men abstain, but only the more serious ones from which the majority can abstain, especially those that harm others and which must be prohibited for human society to survive, such as homicide, theft, and the like" (Sigmund 1988, 54–55).

Political scientist Clarke Cochran interprets Aquinas's adaptation of Aristotelian prudence in the following way:

> Reason, for Aquinas, is rooted in reality, for reason is the acceptance of reality. The soldier in battle has many choices when the grand plans of generals go awry. Some options, which appear courageous, may prove foolhardy. Others, which may appear cowardly, may be brave. No automatic, unswerving principles of right and wrong apply. Rather the virtue of courage—the disposition to choose the courageous action from the multiplicity of possibilities—must draw on prudence for discernment. (Cochran 1991, 50)

Another way to explain the differences between these competing leadership strategies is to say that state university presidents whose curricula completely ignore job training for their students in favor of the arts and sciences are idealists. State university presidents who neither care about the arts and sciences nor require their students to learn about them are cynics. State university presidents who understand the traditional meaning of higher education in the West but emphasize vocational courses in order to increase enrollments and appropriations from state legislatures are pragmatists. And state university presidents who require students to learn how to think critically about their personal lives, their nation, their culture, and the world, even while they are introduced to a trade, are prudent leaders.

In November 1999 a movie entitled *The Insider* was released that focuses on efforts by the Brown and Williamson Tobacco Company to silence one of its former research scientists, Jeffrey Wigand, and prevent the television show *60 Minutes* from airing an interview in which Wigand admitted to celebrated newsman Mike Wallace that tobacco companies fraudulently tamper with nicotine levels to keep smokers addicted to their product. The movie portrays tobacco company executives as cynics for exploiting human beings for profit and for contributing to the death of more than 400,000 Americans annually (Curran 1999, 1A). Wallace and Don Hewitt, *60 Minutes* creator and executive producer, come off as pragmatists who initially consider Wigand's story to be worth telling but who eventually cave in when Brown and Williamson threatens to sue. Radical antismoking crusaders appear as idealists who seem to believe that many of the world's problems will somehow disappear when tobacco is outlawed. Wigand and Lowell Bergman, who produced Wigand's interview with Wallace, are depicted as prudent persons who can see no honorable alternative to taking the heat from Brown and Williamson and the CBS television network and to risking their livelihoods for the sake of the truth.

As philosopher Eugene Garver notes, the difference between prudence and pragmatism is especially difficult to appreciate. "One of the perennial problems of prudence," Garver writes, "is figuring out how to distinguish . . . a virtuous adaptability to circumstances from sophistic accommodation" (Garver 1987, 7). In contrast to pragmatists who define politics as the art of the possible, prudent leaders view it as the art of the preferable. Perhaps George Washington Plunkitt's infamous definitions of honest and dishonest graft can clarify this distinction. Plunkitt of Tammany Hall found a dishonorable way to make it possible for him to get rich at the expense of the people of New York without getting caught and without letting his greed get too far out of control.

Dishonest graft, according to Plunkitt, involves politicians accepting money from "blackmailin' gamblers, saloonkeepers, disorderly people, etc." (Riordan 1963, 3). Honest graft occurs when politicians use insider information to get rich. "Supposin' it's a new bridge they're going to build," Plunkitt says. "I get tipped off and buy as much property as I can that has to be taken for approaches. I sell at my own price later on and drop some money in the bank" (4). Plunkitt's definitions are not cynical because their recognition of limits to political graft indicates that they do not completely abandon moral standards. They are not prudent because they deemphasize morality and the common good. They are pragmatic because they promote self-interest over other considerations when it becomes convenient to do so.

On the basis of this blunt New York machine boss's example, we can learn that it is never prudent for a leader to act in a pragmatic fashion, much less as an idealist or cynic. Yet few leaders are as honest to themselves and as open to others about the true nature of their objectives. In the absence of such candor, scholars attempting to identify prudent policy decisions have no alternative but to incorporate such imprecise tools as hindsight, reading history backward, and making inferences after the fact into their research. Once more we are reminded of the elusiveness of prudence, which was never meant by Aristotle to be easily operationalized either by leaders striving to serve the public interest or scholars searching for handy labels to attach to competing leadership strategies.

A discussion of the storied careers of Robert Leuci and Frank Serpico, two police officers who testified before the 1972 Knapp Commission investigating corruption in the New York City Police Department, presents an additional method for comprehending the distinction between pragmatism and prudence (Fishman 1994a, 200). Leuci, the so-called Prince of the City, was a member of the elite Special Investigating Unit of the department's Narcotics Division. In that position he had daily access to millions of dollars worth of confiscated drugs and drug money. Along the way Leuci and his colleagues sold the drugs, stole the money, and accepted lucrative bribes from drug dealers.

When he was caught by Knapp Commission deputies, Leuci agreed to testify against his colleagues in exchange for immunity from prosecution. He felt like a rat and a stool pigeon, but "deep down he wanted to believe, and he wanted the world to believe, that he had seen evil growing before his eyes, evil that he himself was part of, and he had moved to end it by the only means open to him. He had come forward not as a rat, but as a cop" (Daley 1978, 311). Leuci's behavior in this instance was pragmatic. Like certain state university presidents and like Plunkitt of Tammany Hall, he was motivated primarily by self-interest, but not to the exclusion of some significant moral considerations.

Unlike Leuci, Frank Serpico was scrupulously honest. Confronted by corruption almost from his first day on the job as an undercover officer, he refused to participate. Serpico's refusal was not based on idealism, however, because he would have preferred to ignore his colleagues' lawlessness. He understood that testifying against the offenders would have alienated him from the rest of the force and would have meant the loss of his job (Maas 1973, 82). Yet the option of ignoring the corruption soon was closed to Serpico. He found himself risking life and limb in tracking down and arresting violent criminals, only to see them avoid conviction through a series of payoffs to officers on the take.

At first Serpico was content to tell only his superiors about the graft. When it became clear that they were not at all interested in what he had to say, Serpico approached the *New York Times*, which published a series of articles that led to the formation of the Knapp Commission. This sequence of events caused him to become the very first officer in the history of the New

York Police Department, reputedly the oldest in the United States, to voluntarily testify in a court of law about corruption in the department's ranks. For his efforts, he was shot in the head during a drug investigation under conditions that remain controversial to this day.

Serpico's reaction to the graft epitomizes the principles of Aristotelian prudence. He refused to participate in the corruption itself, but hesitated to testify against corrupt officers because he feared retaliation. When the corruption began to make it impossible for him to do effective police work, however, he concluded that he had to turn the offenders in. Serpico's struggle against lawlessness was thus based on moral ideals, but it did not overlook material circumstances. Critics may object: how can it ever be prudent to risk your job and your life for the sake of an abstract theory of just behavior? Aristotle responds that possession of a soul distinguishes human beings from all other living things. When prudent people find themselves in situations where they simply cannot avoid being directly implicated in serious wrongdoing, they find that nothing is more important to them than preserving the integrity of their souls.

Prudent political leaders also should not be confused with cultural relativists or ideologues. Since Aristotle's theory of prudence posits the existence of universal ideals, it repudiates the claims made by relativists that all values are culturally biased, artificial, and counterfeit. Prudent leaders thus are unable to accept the proposition offered by Thomas Hobbes in 1651 that words such as "good, evil, and contemptible, are ever used with relation to the person that useth them: there being nothing simply and absolutely so; nor any common rule of good or evil, to be taken from the nature of the subjects themselves" (Hobbes 1962, 100).

Since the function of Aristotelian prudence is to reconcile transitory political issues with transcendent political standards, it rejects ideological thinking for advancing one doctrinaire solution to every problem regardless of the circumstances. From the perspective of Aristotle's theory of prudence, therefore, relativists, who discount forever, and ideologues, who overlook today, appear to have engineered simplified, one-dimensional versions of politics based on reductionist views of reality and human nature.

In the eighteenth century Edmund Burke introduced prudence, with its trademark antipathy for relativism and ideology, to the modern Western world. Burke agrees with Aristotle that the primary purpose of politics is to bring "power and right" into harmony (Burke 1955, 71) and that prudence is "the first of all virtues" (71). Like Aristotle, he asserts the relevance of prudent leadership to politics because it allows us to think on the one plane that politics will admit—"on the more or less, the earlier or the later, and on a balance of advantage and inconvenience, of good and evil" (Burke quoted in Canavan 1960, 14).

He also reiterates Aristotle's admonition about the political unsuitability of theoretical reason and the intellectual talents. When abstract ideals are applied to government in a raw condition unfiltered by prudence, Burke warns, flesh and blood human beings will be mistreated and manipulated in the name of these abstractions rather than treated with the dignity that complicated persons who coexist in organic communities deserve. Just as great care must be taken when attempting to transplant bodily organs or transfer vegetation and animals from one environment to another, he argues, utmost caution is required when attempting to transform political systems.

> I flatter myself that I love a manly, moral regulated liberty as well as any gentleman. . . . But I cannot stand forward and give praise or blame to anything which relates to human actions, and human concerns, on a simple view of the object, as it stands stripped of every relation, in all the nakedness and solitude of metaphysical abstraction. Circumstances (which with some gentlemen pass for nothing) give in reality to every political principle its distinguishing color and discriminating effect. The circumstances are what render every civil and political scheme beneficial or noxious to mankind. (Burke 1955, 8)

Unlike cultural relativists, Burke is willing to assert the validity of universal ideals. Unlike ideologues, he disagrees with attempts to apply them indiscriminately everywhere at any time. He opposed the Revolution in France because he felt the French were imposing a doctrine of liberty, equality, and fraternity upon a society historically unprepared to realize such a doctrine. He thus charged the French with practicing politics as if they were computing an algebraic equation and predicted in 1790 that the abstract quality of their venture would usher in a wave of autocratic repression unmatched by the feudal monarchs. Burke favored the American Revolution, however, because in his opinion Americans basically were transplanted Englishmen and -women who were trying merely to adapt traditional English ideals of self-rule to their new home. He considered this to be a prudential goal that would serve to lay a firm foundation for the evolution of republicanism in the United States.

Burke's defense of evolutionary change is based on Aristotle's theory of prudence that cautions against exchanging whatever justice a society has presently achieved for pipe dreams of future perfection. Prudence, Aristotle teaches, involves the integration of a society's present with its past and future through respect for the rule of law. When our ancestors pass down to us specific laws that are patently unjust, the rule of law requires that we amend them as quickly as possible. When we revise laws too frequently, however, we risk denying our descendants the opportunity to enjoy the fruits of justice because they have lost respect for law in general. According to Aristotle:

> All men, as a rule, seek to follow, not the line of tradition, but some idea of the good; and the earliest known human beings . . . were in all probability similar to ordinary or even foolish people today. . . . It would therefore be an absurdity to remain constant to their notions. . . . But while these arguments go to show that in *some* cases, and at *some* times, law ought to be changed, there is another point of view from which it would appear that change is a matter which needs great caution. When we reflect that the improvement likely to be effected may be small, and that it is a bad thing to accustom men to abrogate laws lightheartedly, it becomes clear that there are some defects, both in legislation and in government, which had better be left untouched. (Aristotle 1962, 72–73)

Another common misconception about prudence is that it represents a type of cunning. Cunning implies great skill in discovering the most efficient way to achieve an end whose morality is never seriously considered. Even Mafia hit men can be cunning (Hallowell and Porter 1997, 69). Prudent political leaders, however, cannot divorce themselves from moral principles. They are required to serve the public interest first and foremost and choose means that are commensurate with that goal. Otherwise their behavior becomes "mere clever roguery" (Ross 1960, 214).

The contrast between cunning and prudence is clarified by the practice of realpolitik in foreign affairs. Proponents of realpolitik, such as the nineteenth-century Austrian diplomat Prince Klemens von Metternich, dedicate themselves to the maintenance of the status quo by manipulating the perpetually shifting international balance of power. Metternich sought short-term solutions to international problems without considering the implications of those solutions either for the ideal of justice or the long-term interests of the nations involved. He believed in balance of power as an end in itself that justifies whatever means diplomats have at their disposal. In short, he substituted "tactical virtuosity" or cunning for the artful mix of ethical norms and circumstances that defines Aristotelian prudence (Bill 1997, 217).

Prudent leaders consider ideals to be necessary but insufficient for politics (Canavan 1960, 25). They judge ideals to be necessary because ideals provide infallible goals of justice toward which fallible human beings who

tend to be unjust can strive. They judge ideals to be insufficient because ideals are unable to adjust themselves to the constantly changing complex demands and challenges of everyday life. From this perspective, prudent
leaders emerge as authentic realists in their quest to balance the immaterial
and material aspects of the universe, the good and bad impulses of human
beings, and the theory and practice of politics.

The scope and magnitude of prudential realism find expression in the
thought of the twentieth-century neo-Thomist Jacques Maritain. Maritain,
who lived and wrote during the Nazi Holocaust, located in the theory of
prudence justification for the temporary use of otherwise unjust methods
by otherwise just people to overthrow Hitler. "The application of moral
rules immutable in themselves takes lower and lower forms as the social
environment declines," Maritain argues:

> In utterly barbarized societies like a concentration camp, or even in
> quite particular conditions like those of clandestine resistance in an
> occupied country, many things which were, as to their moral nature,
> objectively fraud or murder or perfidy in ordinary civilized life cease,
> now, to come under the same definition and become . . . objectively
> permissible or ethical things. (Maritain 1951, 73)

If the general philosophic purpose of prudence is to reconcile the transcendent with the transitory, the immutable with the imminent, and forever with today, its specific political function is to impart vision to the
formulation of public policy. As Proverbs 29:18 teaches, "Where there is no
vision, the people perish." While many politicians in democracies pass
laws solely to please temporary majorities of voters, prudential democratic
leaders design policies for the organic community of voters consisting, in
journalist Walter Lippmann's words, of "the entire living population, with
their predecessors and successors" (Lippmann 1955, 32). To Lippmann,
prudent leadership is comparable to the impulse that persuades young
people to "die in battle for their country" and older ones "to plant trees they
will never sit under" (35).

It is also necessary to distinguish between prudence and judgment and
to discuss the relationship between prudence and character. Although prudence involves good judgment, it demands that judgment be manifested in
action or praxis. For this reason Aquinas defines prudence as the "right reason of doing" (Pieper 1959, 29). "If I see what the situation requires, but am
unable to bring myself to act in a manner befitting my understanding,"
Ronald Beiner writes, "I possess judgment but not *phronesis*." Prudence,

therefore, "is judgment consummated in the efficacy of good *praxis*" (Beiner 1983, 74).

Aristotle, furthermore, upholds personal moral character as a prerequisite for political prudence. Human beings, he argues, cannot be expected to provide prudent leadership, that is, virtuous leadership, unless they are already virtuous themselves. "Virtuous actions are not done in a virtuous—a just or temperate—way merely because *they* have the appropriate quality," he writes. "The *doer* must be in a certain frame of mind when he does them" (Aristotle 1966, 61). Since Aristotle is quite aware of human pride, greed, and selfishness, however, he cannot require prudent leaders to be wholly without sin—only that they honestly strive to act with as much common decency as possible. The standard of virtue by which he evaluates leaders applies to lifetime behavior patterns, not to isolated acts of human weakness that may have been performed while in or out of office.

As philosopher Joseph Dunne observes, "Aristotelian *phronesis*, more than simply directing us to the love of good action, is itself already the fruit of a life devoted to the love of good action" (Dunne 1993, 310). On this point, indeed, Aristotle is adamant: it is possible to be personally virtuous and fail as a political leader, he insists, but impossible to succeed at political leadership without the type of personal virtue to which people become habituated over the course of their lives. According to Aristotle:

> If a man possesses the two qualifications of capacity and loyalty to the constitution, is there any need for him to have the third qualification of goodness, and will not the first two, by themselves, secure the public interest? We may answer this question by asking another. May not men who possess these first two qualifications be unable to command their passions? and is it not true that men who have no command of their passions will fail to serve their own interest—even though they possess self-knowledge and self-loyalty—and will equally fail to serve the public interest (even though they possess a knowledge of public affairs and public loyalty)? (Aristotle 1962, 231)

An Aristotelian *phronimos*, or expert practitioner of political prudence, is a member of that group of persons Aristotle classifies as "great-souled men" for whom personal virtue "is a *sine qua non*" (Aristotle 1966, 123). What is meant by personal virtue? To Aristotle it represents the ability to practice moderation in the fulfillment of our animal passions by not permitting the passions to lose sight of the higher human purposes they are intended to serve—that is, by not letting them become ends in themselves. "The man who is passion's slave" is immoderate and thus unjust, he writes (310). Aristotle clearly is no prude. He teaches that the food we consume might as well be delicious as long as we remember that we eat to live, not live to eat. The sex we have might as well be exciting as long as we understand that sexual relations are an intimate expression of love, not a cheap form of pleasure. Similarly, the quest for political power can be commendable as long as we use power primarily to serve others, not just ourselves.

Aristotle expected his concept of prudence to serve as a paradigm toward which political leaders should strive but which not even the most effective leaders could always realize. Because it involves the most precarious of political skills, "knowledge of the correct ends or values as well as the calculation of the correct means to these ends" (Mulgan 1977, 9), there is a significant element of uncertainty in prudence. According to historian James Bill:

> the practice of prudence is often fragile and fleeting. No statesman practices it to perfection. All leaders have weaknesses and make mistakes. They can easily lose sight of their moral goals; moral vision can slip into moralism and polemicism; the means can become ends in themselves; and the temptation to vanity is ever present. The statesman's knowledge and understanding may be imbalanced and imperfect and, if unwilling to admit this, the leader may not recruit the necessary expertise. (Bill 1997, 228)

Bill here refers to internal factors that mitigate against practicing prudence successfully. But there are external impediments as well, including some very powerful groups with selfish interests they long to satisfy and enormously intricate national and international forces that may or may not be amenable to change. "The certitude of prudence," Aquinas thus writes, "cannot be so great as completely to remove all anxiety" (Aquinas quoted in Pieper 1959, 18). In view of these obstacles, Aristotle concludes that there is an element of what may be termed "moral luck" inherent in *phronesis* (Nussbaum 1986, xiv). The author of Ecclesiastes 9:11 reaches a similar conclusion: "I returned and saw under the sun that the race is not to the swift, nor the battle to the strong, neither yet bread to the wise nor riches to men of understanding, but time and chance happeneth to them all."

To the question of what can be done to harness "moral luck" and cause it to operate in the service of the public interest, Aristotle responds that reason alone cannot suffice. A certain amount of intuition or what philosopher Michael Polanyi calls "tacit knowledge" also is required. "It appears, then," Polanyi writes, "that to know that a statement is true is to know more than we can tell and that, hence, when a discovery solves a problem, it is itself fraught with further intimations of an indeterminate range, and that furthermore, when we accept the discovery as true, we commit ourselves to a

belief in all these as yet undisclosed, perhaps as yet unthinkable, consequences" (Polanyi 1967, 23).

Given its explicit reliance on ideals, luck, and tacit knowledge, *phronesis*
does not claim to be a method that analyzes decisions in a neutral, objective
manner. "The essence of leadership," anthropologist F. G. Bailey thus argues, "obliterates the scientific search for objective fact" (Bailey 1988, 4).
For Aristotle, indeed, the personal values of leaders constitute an ineludta-
ble aspect of the policy-making process. As he makes clear on the very first
line of his *Politics*: Despite what many may think, human beings are not
mechanical calculators of cold, hard data. Everything that each one of us
thinks and does is influenced by the values to which we consciously or unconsciously ascribe (Aristotle 1962, 1).

Of course, Aristotle cannot guarantee that any combination of realistic
values, rational planning, and intuition always will result in prudent policies. As he well knew, even Pericles ultimately was defeated by conditions
and events beyond his control. Having decided to abandon a direct counterattack against the Spartan siege of Athens in favor of a defensive strategy, a deadly plague engulfed the city, killing a third of its inhabitants
including Pericles himself. In view of Pericles' own experiences, Aristotle
cautions leaders that those who hold public office have a responsibility to
serve the public interest that is neither excused nor relieved when their best
efforts prove inadequate.

Nor is prudence the equivalent of compromise. When political leaders
act prudently, they are able to reconcile immutable abstract ideals with
variable concrete circumstances. But while these reconciliations bear some
resemblance to compromise, they are made for the express purpose of serving a higher end, namely, the public interest, not for the sake of compromise
itself. As Eugene Garver writes, "prudence is not simply the middle
ground between two extremes" (Garver 1987, 19).

According to John Hallowell:

Although politics comes into being as a result of the conflict of wills
and interests it presupposes the existence of certain interests and values in common, for without this basis for reconciliation there could be
no politics. Politics has sometimes been defined as the technique of
compromise. This is both true and false. It is false if the end of politics
is thought to be compromise for its own sake, but it is true to the extent
that compromise presupposes some agreement upon principles in
terms of which compromise may take place. No one likes compromise for its own sake and no political society could be based on love of
compromise. Persons are willing to make compromises only because
they value some things more than they do the things which they are

compromising. When a society no longer values common interests above personal interests the society disintegrates, compromise is no longer possible and politics ceases. (Hallowell 1950, 5–6)

Has presidential behavior occasionally conformed to the standards of what Aristotle means by *phronesis*? The following chapter contains specific examples of presidents not only comprehending the universal ideals that infuse human existence with purpose and direction but also demonstrating the flexibility to reconcile universal ideals with the diverse political pressures that confronted the United States while they were in office. At least on these occasions during the course of American history, presidents provided the kind of prudent leadership that evokes the memory of Pericles and elevates them to the status of an Aristotelian *phronimos*.

---------------- CHAPTER 3 ----------------

Prudent Presidential
Leadership

ABRAHAM LINCOLN, SLAVERY, AND THE CIVIL WAR

Central to Aristotelian prudence are a dedication to principle, an appreciation of circumstance, and an ability to blend the two. It represents a balance between "an ethics of principle, in which those principles univocally dictate action . . . and an ethics of consequences, in which the successful result is all" (Garver 1987, 12). Abraham Lincoln often succeeded in striking this sort of balance both in his attitude toward slavery and in the way he conducted the Civil War.

Lincoln's position on slavery echoes Aristotle, who supported the institution but condemned slavery of a race based on conquest. Since proponents of prudent leadership assume that we as human beings have souls that provide us with the power to choose, they are led to conclude that we require at least some significant degree of political freedom in order to exercise our humanity. As Lincoln put it: "If the Negro is a man, is it not to that extent, a total destruction of self-government, to say that he too shall not govern himself?" (Current 1967, 72).

Concerning slavery in principle, Lincoln was unequivocal. "I am naturally anti-slavery," he wrote in 1864. "If slavery is not wrong, nothing is wrong. I can not remember when I did not so think, and feel" (297). Before 1861, however, he opposed the idea put forth by some radical abolitionists to utilize the power of the national government to end slavery in the South. To compel Southerners to overturn ingrained social, economic, and political practices that had existed among them for 200 years, he reasoned, would produce a level of chaos much worse than the status quo for everyone concerned, including the slaves themselves. Because Lincoln believed that technological changes would render slavery anachronistic in the near future, he recommended that it be permitted to die a natural death in the South over time (Fishman 1994b, 7).

Lincoln also was unable to support Stephen Douglas's plan to allow local plebiscites to extend slavery to the territories, where the South's "peculiar institution" had not taken root and the principles of liberty and equality enjoyed far greater acceptance. Democracy, Lincoln insisted, does not extend to the majority the right to deny people their democratic birthrights. As he said in the famous Lincoln-Douglas debates:

> The Republican Party . . . looks upon (slavery) as being a moral, social and political wrong; and while they contemplate it as such, they nevertheless have due regard for its actual existence among us, and the difficulties of getting rid of it in any satisfactory way. . . . Yet having due regard for these, they desire a policy in regard to it that looks to its not creating any more danger. They insist that it should as far as may be, *be treated* as a wrong, and one of the methods of treating it as wrong is to *make provision that it shall grow no larger*. (Current 1967, 110)

When South Carolina laid siege to Fort Sumter, Lincoln's prudence again was put to the test. The secessionists claimed they were merely acting to protect states' rights against the national government. Lincoln, thinking ahead to how important public opinion would be to the Northern war effort, sought to immediately shift the burden of aggression over to the rebels. Toward that end he formally announced his intention to send medicine and food by barge to the besieged troops. When the rebels fired on the unarmed convoy, as Lincoln knew they would, his public opinion ploy prevailed. Once more principle and circumstance, coming to the aid of injured and starving persons as a pretext to war, achieved their necessary balance.

With the outbreak of full-scale fighting, Lincoln felt obliged to explain why Northern soldiers should risk their lives in battle against other Americans. Saving the Union may be an effective war cry, but it smacks of jingoism and thus is insufficiently principled to satisfy the standards of prudent political leadership. Lincoln solved this dilemma by connecting the Union to the ideals it represents, namely, freedom and equality under the law. To attack the Union, he maintained, was to attack its most basic ideals. To save the Union was to preserve these ideals for the rest of the world to emulate. Lincoln first articulated this view in 1854 while opposing the Kansas-Nebraska Act.

> This *declared* indifference, but as I must think, covert real zeal for the spread of slavery, I can not but hate. I hate it because of the monstrous injustice of slavery itself. I hate it because it deprives our republican example of its just influence in the world—enables the enemies of free institutions, with plausibility, to taunt us as hypocrites—causes the real friends of freedom to doubt our sincerity, and especially because it forces so many really good men amongst ourselves into an open war with the very fundamental principles of civil liberty—criticizing the Declaration of Independence, and insisting that there is no right principle of action but self-interest. (326–27)

Without denying his repugnance for slavery and desire to see it eradicated as soon as possible, Lincoln now became committed to winning the war as his number one priority. New circumstances warrant new policies, he explained to journalist Horace Greeley in 1862. "My paramount object in this struggle *is* to save the Union, and is *not* either to save or to destroy slavery. If I could save the Union without freeing *any* slave I would do it, and if I could save it by freeing *all* the slaves I would do it; and if I could save it by freeing some and leaving others alone I would also do that" (215).

Fearful of losing the loyalty of the border states at a time when Union forces were on the defensive, Lincoln countermanded an 1861 order by General John C. Fremont to free slaves in Missouri. Two years later, however, he reacted to the prospect of victory by employing a new strategy. On January 1, 1863, he issued the Emancipation Proclamation, which had the practical effect of freeing Confederate slaves alone. True to his prudential purposes, Lincoln wanted to espouse the nation's opposition to slavery in dramatic terms while keeping the border states on his side and encouraging Confederate slaves to take up arms against their masters.

Was it not now inconsistent for Lincoln to abolish slavery in the South when he had explicitly opposed that course of action before the North started winning battles? His previous position had been that overturning a long established institution too quickly would lead to societal chaos reminiscent of France after its revolution. But once the Southern states brought chaos upon themselves, and the border states chose to side with a winner, extreme caution was no longer necessary. The principles remained the same, freedom and equality under the law. When historical circumstances changed, new, less conciliatory policies became possible.

Throughout the war Lincoln resorted to methods that led some to charge him with being a "presidential dictator." Among the extra-legal powers he assumed were to raise an army without congressional consent, suspend the writ of habeas corpus, permit government tampering with private correspondence, and declare martial law behind the lines. While admitting the unconstitutionality of these actions, Lincoln claimed they were made necessary by an extraordinary challenge to the Constitution itself. "I did understand," he explained in 1864,

> that my oath to preserve the constitution to the best of my ability, imposed upon me the duty of preserving, by every indispensable means, that government—that nation—of which that constitution was the organic law. Was it possible to lose the nation, and yet preserve the constitution? By general law life and limb must be protected; yet often a limb must be amputated to save a life; but a life is never wisely given to save a limb. I felt that measures, otherwise unconstitutional, might become lawful, by becoming indispensable to the preservation of the constitution, through the preservation of the nation. Right or wrong, I assumed this ground, and now avow it. (298)

Lincoln pursued peace with the same intensity that he directed the fighting. In his 1865 inaugural address he called for a Reconstruction process featuring "malice toward none . . . charity for all" (316). In opposition to the radicals of his own party, he proposed a "Ten Percent Plan" that would restore any Confederate state to the Union once one-tenth of its citizens who had voted in the 1860 presidential election pledged their allegiance to the Constitution. After Appomattox he refused to execute any of the rebels and only briefly imprisoned a few, including Jefferson Davis. He endorsed passage of the Thirteenth Amendment and supported efforts by agencies such as the Freedmen's Bureau to aid former slaves.

Given the difficulty people have in comprehending policies that defy ideological stereotypes and in distinguishing between prudence and competing leadership strategies, it is not surprising that Lincoln's positions on slavery and the Civil War were widely misinterpreted. Despite his unequivocal opposition to human bondage, Radical Republicans condemned him as a "slavehound." Despite his antebellum pledge to prevent the national government from interfering with slavery, Southern Democrats denounced him as an abolitionist. Perhaps the unkindest cut came from Stephen Douglas, who characterized him as an enemy of popular sovereignty. In his masterful study of the Lincoln-Douglas debates, *Crisis of the House Divided*, political scientist Harry Jaffa attempts to explain the misguided nature of these charges. What confused Lincoln's critics and fanned the flames of their vituperation, Jaffa argues, was the novelty of his belief that "changing circumstances might reasonably elicit constructive interpretations of old principles" (Jaffa 1982, 12).

There were numerous policy orientations available to Lincoln as he confronted the disintegration of the United States over the issue of slavery. He could have upheld the idealistic position lauded by radicals such as John Brown that "every man, woman, and child then living should meet violent death" for violating even " 'one word' of the Golden Rule or the Declaration of Independence" (Blum, Morgan et al. 1977, 312). He could have gone along with Stephen Douglas's version of popular sovereignty that represents the essence of pragmatism since it neglects to pay sufficient attention to the moral implications of slavery. He could have found a way to cynically exploit the turmoil for his own political advantage. Or he could have exerted prudent leadership by adjusting to the frightful events swirling around him without allowing himself to be overwhelmed by them.

According to Jaffa, Lincoln "understood the task of statesmanship . . . to know what is good or right, to know how much of that good is attainable, and to act to secure that much good but not to abandon the attainable good by grasping for more" (371). His policies, Jaffa writes, "pointed simultaneously in two directions: one, towards the philosopher's understanding of the universal, transpolitical dimension of human experience; the other, towards the political man's understanding of the particular experiences of particular peoples in particular regimes" (1). Herein lies the connection between Lincoln's politics and Aristotle's philosophy, Jaffa maintains. Both "undertook to guide political men, who need to know what is right here and now, but to guide them in the light of what is just everywhere and always" (1).

GEORGE WASHINGTON AND THE NATION'S FOUNDING

Another critical aspect of Aristotelian prudence is its distinctive view of human nature that both approves of and harbors suspicion about the power of the soul to make commendable decisions. George Washington displayed that view in his approach to the nation's founding. For centuries prior to Washington's inauguration in 1789, political philosophers considered popular government to be inherently unstable. It was widely held that citizens of republics first would pursue freedom to excess, soon grow tired of fulfilling the responsibilities of self-rule, and later solicit tyrants to contend with the resulting chaos by imposing their own brand of oppressive discipline.

The political climate that prevailed during the early days of American independence seemed to confirm this pessimistic assessment. A century and a half of life marked by self-sufficiency on the frontier had persuaded many Americans that individuals could govern themselves without much interference from formal political institutions. The inept rule of George III and the British Parliament made them particularly suspicious of centralized authority. Typically during the period between 1776 and 1781, governors were chosen by state legislatures, shared power with executive councils, and often served one-year terms (Thomas, Pika, and Watson 1994, 17). After 1781 the Articles of Confederation decentralized and fragmented American national government to the point of impotence. In the confusion that followed, demagogues such as Daniel Shays began to attract mass support.

When the new Constitution was ratified in 1788, Washington was probably the only representative of the established order to whom Americans would delegate any significant amount of power. The courage, honesty, diligence and acumen with which he had fought the Revolution dispelled fear on the part of his countrymen and -women that he would abuse their trust. When Washington became chief executive, their trust in him was transferred to the government. When he achieved success in office, popular endorsement for republicanism was guaranteed. Americans started to appreciate the handiwork of Washington and the other Founding Fathers who had designed a political system at the Philadelphia Constitutional Convention of 1787 that simultaneously was weak enough to permit popular sovereignty and strong enough to combat anarchy. Washington, political scientist Seymour Martin Lipset writes, served as a "symbol of the new nation, its hero who embodies in his person its values and aspirations. But more than merely symbolizing the new nation, he legitimized the state, the new secular government, by endowing it with his 'gift of grace'" (Lipset 1979, 18).

On the one hand, Washington believed in the ideals of individualism and equality. He summarily rejected a request by Continental Army officers that he become king. On the other hand, Washington recognized that, in order to ensure the future prospects of newly established republics where an emphasis on liberty already exists, it is necessary to temper that liberty with a prudent amount of political authority. He wanted to show Americans, in other words, that "the head of a state can be powerful without endangering liberty" (Dallek 1996, 11). "We have probably had too good an opinion of human nature in forming our confederation," Washington wrote in familiar Aristotelian terms. "Experience has taught us, that men will not adopt and carry into execution measures the best calculated for their own good without the intervention of a coercive power" (Washington quoted in Morgan 1980, 80).

Even Thomas Jefferson, who was prone to distrust Washington's commitment to republicanism and expressed support for a more decentralized national government that would allow Americans a greater degree of individual freedom, had to admit that Washington's vindication of political power in those early years delivered the United States from "a subversion of that liberty it was intended to establish" (Jefferson quoted in Flexner 1974, 175). According to Jefferson, "Perhaps the strongest feature in his character was prudence, never acting until every circumstance, every consideration, was maturely weighed. . . . His integrity was most pure, his justice the most inflexible I have ever known" (Jefferson quoted in Hughes 1973, 50).

One of the notable issues over which Washington exercised authority was American foreign policy. After Louis XVI was guillotined in January 1793 and hostilities ensued between England and France, there existed a considerable difference of opinion in the United States over what would constitute an appropriate official approach to the belligerents. The pro-French Democratic-Republican societies maintained that, in light of our more closely held republican values and because of their crucial support during our own struggle with England, the United States had a moral duty to honor the mutual defense treaties we had signed with France in 1778. Secretary of the Treasury Alexander Hamilton represented those factions that favored England out of fear of its formidable navy and because it constituted a more valuable trading partner. Secretary of State Jefferson recommended a pragmatic point of view. The United States could gain greater concessions from England in return for a formal declaration of neutrality at a later date, he explained, if it stayed out of the war without initially declaring its official intentions.

Washington felt otherwise. While the United States was politically, economically, and militarily weak and in the process of struggling to get its domestic house in order, he argued, it would be imprudent to become entangled in international affairs. In April 1793 he issued a Neutrality Proclamation that continues to serve as a model for the foreign policy of new nations. According to Washington, the United States had the right to expect other countries to refrain from interfering with American sovereignty, and the concomitant obligation to prohibit American citizens from interfering with the sovereignty of other countries (Malone and Rauch 1960a, 38).

Washington's proclamation gave rise to a constitutional debate concerning the power of presidents to make such foreign policy decisions. Jefferson and James Madison argued that Congress has the right to formulate foreign policy by virtue of the power to declare war delegated to it in Article I Section 8 of the Constitution. Washington and Hamilton nevertheless were able to persuade the American people and Congress itself that the broad grant of executive power found in Article II Section 1 creates "a concurrent authority" between the president and Congress in the field of foreign affairs (Hamilton quoted in Corwin 1957, 179).

If Washington had been an idealist during these times and in these policy areas, his positions would have been closer to Jeffersonian egalitarianism. Had he been a pragmatist, he would have paid even greater attention to British interests. Had he been a cynic, he would have accepted the offer to become king. That Washington chose the alternative of prudent leadership is reflected in the remarks of United States Supreme Court Chief Justice John Marshall. "Endowed by nature with a sound judgment, and an accurate and discriminating mind," Marshall writes of Washington,

> he feared not that laborious attention which made him perfectly master of those subjects, in all their relations, on which he was to decide; and this essential quality was guided by an unvarying sense of moral right, which would tolerate the employment only of those means that would bear the most rigid examination; by a fairness of intention which neither sought nor required disguise; and a purity of virtue which not only was untainted, but unsuspected. (Marshall quoted in Freeman 1968, xii)

THEODORE ROOSEVELT AND CONSERVATION

Although it harbors no illusions about what can be accomplished, Aristotelian prudence requires political leaders to do their very best to keep at least some semblance of responsible human behavior alive in a world often subsumed by greed. In the early twentieth century Theodore Roosevelt applied this aspect of prudential realism to the issue of conservation.

The ideal TR applied to nature is the biblical injunction that we have dominion over the earth. Although the word "dominion" means to have power over or to control, it also requires that we assume responsibility for our power. We have inherited the earth. It remains available for our use. But we do have to pass it down to our children and our children's children in at least as good shape as we received it (Fishman 1998, 4).

While acknowledging that it is never acceptable to exploit nature, TR nevertheless recognized that before the twentieth century it would have been unrealistic to expect the national government to prevent it. During that time democracy in the United States was considered to be synonymous with extraordinary self-sufficiency. TR was quite an individualist himself, but he concluded that damage to the environment had gone too far. In order for future generations to enjoy their fair share of American natural resources, he argued, priority would have to be given to the public interest over special interests. In order to restrain these powerful special interests, government intervention was necessary. Because natural resources extend beyond state boundaries, the national government would have to set most of the restraints (Harbaugh 1975, 318).

In fact TR was the first president to establish a coherent national conservation program for the United States (Wilson 1971, 154). His initial order of business involved land reclamation. In 1902 he signed the Newlands Reclamation Act, which brought irrigation to arid acreage in the American West and turned expanses of waste regions into productive farmland. The act financed the construction of public projects, such as the 260-foot-high Roosevelt Dam in Arizona, which supplied water to local farmers whose fees for the service were reinvested for future undertakings (Cutright 1956, 168).

TR then moved to protect American forests. When he took office four-fifths of the timber in the United States was privately owned. Of that total, one-half was controlled by 200 holders, most notably the Southern Pacific Railway, the Northern Pacific Railway, and the Weyerhaeuser Timber Company (Roosevelt 1913, 456). In 1905 TR sought to democratize this situation by quadrupling the size of the national forests, transferring their care from the Department of the Interior to the Department of Agriculture, and creating the United States Forest Service with the famed conservationist Gifford Pinchot as its head. On Pinchot's recommendation, he insisted that national preserves be administered according to the scientific principles of selective harvesting and reforestation and that people who grazed their livestock there or otherwise utilized them for profit pay fair charges for the privilege (Malone and Rauch 1960b, 222).

Next came the issue of national monuments and parks. In 1906 TR persuaded Congress to pass the National Monuments Act, which led to the development of such magnificent sites as Wyoming's Devil Tower, California's Muir Woods, and Arizona's Petrified Forest, and Grand Canyon. Although Congress reserved for itself the power to create national parks, TR used his influence to establish Oregon's Crater Lake, Oklahoma's Platt National Park, South Dakota's Wind Cave, North Dakota's Sully Hill, and Colorado's Mesa Verde (Harbaugh 1975, 315).

Concerning plants and animals, TR's efforts led to the establishment of fifty-one wildlife preserves in every part of the country. The first of these was on Florida's Pelican Island where hunters were prohibited from exterminating beautifully plumed birds for the sake of the fashion industry (Cutright 1956, 178).

In 1908, moreover, TR appointed a special federal commission to cooperate with state officials for the purpose of compiling a complete inventory of American natural resources, including mineral and ore deposits. His goal was to effect a balance between the right of Americans to make a living through mastery of nature today and our moral duty to protect the earth for generations to come. Through scientific analysis of the environment, he maintained, we would be able to calculate what could be spared for present appropriation and what should be saved for the future (Harbaugh 1975, 319).

Perhaps TR's greatest contribution to the field of conservation was the publicity he gave to the cause. Through innumerable speeches and publications he strived to educate Americans that nature is not inexhaustible and that the continued abuse of its bounty would be tantamount to killing the goose that laid the golden egg. The culmination of his publicity campaign took place in 1908 when he called the Governor's Conference on Conservation at the White House. There he challenged leading federal and state officials, scientists, and influential private individuals such as Andrew Carnegie and James T. Hill to help bring about an end to the era in which a minority of Americans used laissez-faire economics to justify their plunder of the environment (Malone and Rauch 1960b, 223).

The final measure of TR's prudence in the area of conservation derived from his ability to preserve nature's riches against special interests with opposing agendas who dominated Congress. Prior to Roosevelt's administrations, there were few laws and policies of any kind on any level of government that kept private industries trading in such commodities as wood, railroads, utilities, livestock, oil, and coal from monopolizing and decimating the country's natural resources.

When TR challenged their dominance, these industries tried to use the members of Congress they controlled to denounce him and block his initiatives. In one historic incident Congress passed an agricultural bill that severely limited the amount of land TR could set aside as national forests. Roosevelt's response was to work behind the scenes to save 16,000,000 additional acres just before the bill officially became law (Roosevelt 1913, 440). Of course, his efforts were not always so successful. Upon leaving office his hand-picked successor, William Howard Taft, succumbed to the pressure exerted by the special interests to fire Pinchot and other like-minded federal administrators and dismantle many of their programs.

Although TR emphasized moral ideals, like Aristotle he recognized that ideals alone are insufficient for politics. He was a dedicated naturalist, but he also appreciated the passion with which Americans reserve for themselves the right to make a profit. In order to prevent the further decimation of our natural resources, he proposed a prudent reconciliation between environmentalism and free enterprise. Like Aristotle, moreover, TR rejected both relativism and ideology. His environmental policy provides a prudent alternative to the exploiters of nature and doctrinaire environmentalists. While the former make the fatal mistake of loving nature too little, he maintained, the latter commit the equally serious error of loving it well beyond the limits of science and common sense.

Had TR adopted an idealistic approach to conservation he would have been willing to subvert all aspects of American life, including the advantages of industrialization and the profit motive, in favor of doctrinaire environmentalism. When these ideologues accused him of hypocrisy for promoting conservation while being an avid hunter, he replied:

> tho emphatically against game butchery, or any other kind of butchery of wild things, and emphatically in favor of the preservation of all wild life that can be preserved without detriment to mankind, I still do feel, not only that there is no objection to a reasonable amount of hunting, but that the encouragement of a proper hunting spirit, a proper love of sport, instead of being incompatible with a love of nature and wild things, offers the best guaranty for the preservation of wild things. (Morison 1952, 1125)

Had TR been a pragmatist, on the other hand, he would have made even more concessions to the industrialists than he did make. Had he been a cynic, he would have totally succumbed to the crass materialism and greed that defined so much of the "Gilded Age" into which he was born.

Instead, TR's specific approach to conservation was based on a general attitude toward politics that he described as "applied idealism" (Roosevelt 1913, 144). He expressed "profound anger and contempt alike for the malicious impractical visionary . . . and for the vicious and cynical professional politicians" (Roosevelt quoted in Blum 1967, 12). His distinctive alternative was a politics "born of conviction as well as expediency," a "hodgepodge compounded of the ideal and the practicable" (17). Almost a century ago Theodore Roosevelt instituted programs that were designed to save the environment for present and future generations. Today, when we visit a national park or take our grandchildren to enjoy a wildlife preserve, we bear witness to his prudent leadership.

FRANKLIN D. ROOSEVELT AND FOREIGN POLICY

By Aristotle's estimation prudent leadership depends in part on policy choices that are a product of a leader's intuition. For Aristotle, moreover, the success of a leader's intuitive decisions depends to a certain extent on moral luck. The manner in which Franklin Delano Roosevelt executed his foreign policy initiatives illustrates the roles that intuition and moral luck play in effective political leadership.

The international scene FDR encountered when he became president hovered on the brink of total war. Through foreign policy FDR sought to achieve Woodrow Wilson's ideal of helping to create a world in which independent democratic governments, representing themselves in a vital international peace organization, could flourish. The obstacles to this goal were manifold. He had to confront the heritage of American neutrality that extended back to Washington's decision in 1793 to avoid foreign entanglements. Adding to his troubles was the animosity of the Axis powers to democracy and the desire of many of our allies to maintain their extensive colonial empires (Fishman 1997, 156).

Against the isolationists in his own country, who accused him of being a warmonger intent on provoking war with the Axis powers, FDR argued that the twentieth century represented a radical break with the past. Technological innovations in transportation and communication had created a world in which people and nations were interrelated to a degree previously unknown. National and international crises occurred more frequently and with greater complexity than ever before. Multinational pressure groups were being organized to promote the selfish interests of a privileged few. Under these novel conditions, FDR maintained, our historic reliance on isolationism had become anachronistic. His position was that unprecedented times create unprecedented problems that, in turn, require unprecedented solutions. Washington's policy was undoubtedly appropriate for its time. But for the United States in the modern world, he concluded, there is no viable alternative to energetic participation in international affairs.

Despite his endorsement of a more active role for the United States in world politics, FDR was determined not to become a Wilsonian idealist on the subject. Nor did he favor the pursuit of a cynical policy of realpolitik that would manipulate the international scene to favor American interests or a pragmatic approach dedicated to what would be convenient for the United States. According to Erwin Hargrove, his "views on international relations were a blend of the realism of Theodore Roosevelt, who recognized the importance of national power in a lawless world, and the idealism of Woodrow Wilson, who envisioned the United States as the apostle of peace and law among nations" (Hargrove 1998, 101).

In reference to the difficult balancing act involving ideals and material circumstances that prudent leaders must perform in conducting foreign policy, FDR described himself as a "juggler" (Goodwin 1994, 137). He also liked to compare his job to that of a football quarterback (Burns 1970, 295). The universal ideal constituted his pregame plan. He would make a policy decision or call a play in the huddle based on that plan, he said, and then feel free to change the policy or call an audible at the line of scrimmage depending on the specific defensive formation he encountered.

His first critical foreign policy test came during the period between the Nazi invasion of Poland and the Japanese attack on Pearl Harbor when Americans had not yet accepted the inevitability of their entrance into the war. In order to fortify the Allies while he educated American public opinion about the nature of the Axis threat, he cut off trade with Japan, traded aged destroyers for British air and naval bases in the Western hemisphere, protected British convoys against German submarines in the North Atlantic, and invented the lend-lease plan. The purpose of lend-lease, he told a national audience in a December 1940 "Fireside Chat," was for the United States to become the "great arsenal of democracy" by producing ships, planes, and guns to ensure an Allied victory in Europe (FDR quoted in Goodwin 1994, 194).

When Germany invaded the Soviet Union in 1941 FDR again confounded the isolationists by his insistence on extending lend-lease to the Russians. As opposed to those Americans who would have preferred to see Hitler destroy Stalin, FDR realized that the longer the Russians held out, the longer we would have to mobilize. Since the United States at the time possessed almost no modern weapons and only a limited supply of antiquated ones, the prescient quality of his decision to share what little we had with the Allies becomes even more remarkable.

While FDR continued to be frustrated by his inability to convince Americans that mobilization was necessary and that the war was worth fighting, the Japanese struck. Talk about moral luck! "As it were," historian Patrick Maney notes, "Pearl Harbor rallied and united the American people to an extent that even Roosevelt could never have equalled. Even in tragedy, it seemed, his luck had held" (Maney 1992, 139).

After Pearl Harbor FDR had to face the issue of competing battlefronts. Many Americans assumed that, since we had been attacked by the Japanese, we ought to concentrate our efforts in the Pacific. But FDR knew better. He instinctively realized that Germany, with its control over most of Europe, interest in Latin America, and superior technological capability, presented a greater threat to the United States and had to be defeated first.

FDR's position on American war aims remained consistent until his death in 1945. In January 1941 he described for Congress his vision of a postwar world "founded upon four essential freedoms," freedom of speech and expression, freedom of religion, freedom from want, and freedom from fear

(Roosevelt quoted in Freidel 1990, 361). In August 1941 he secured Winston Churchill's reluctant acceptance of the "Atlantic Charter," dedicated to world peace through national self-determination and equal access to trade and raw materials.

In March 1944 he told reporters that we were "fighting to make a world in which tyranny and aggression cannot exist; a world based upon freedom, equality, and justice; a world in which all persons regardless of race, color, or creed may live in peace, honor, and dignity" (FDR quoted in Burns 1970, 468). From August through September 1944 he hosted a meeting of Allied representatives at Dumbarton Oaks in Washington, D.C., to plan for the formation of a permanent international peace organization. And at Yalta in February 1945 he arranged for a conference to be held in San Francisco to establish the United Nations.

As an idealist FDR would have tried, like Wilson, to move far beyond American public opinion on the questions of declaring war, military strategy, and postwar aims. As a pragmatist, he would have rejected plans to come to the aid of the Allies and passively waited for the Axis powers to declare war on the United States. As a cynic, he would have joined the ranks of the extreme isolationists and lent implicit American support to the Nazi attack on the Soviet Union and worldwide communism.

Historian Arthur Schlesinger, Jr., Rexford Tugwell, a member of the group of FDR advisers known as the "Brains Trust," and Frances Perkins, the woman he appointed as secretary of labor, observe that the method FDR utilized to reject these idealistic, pragmatic, and cynical policy alternatives involved a component of the very intuitiveness Aristotle notes must play a role in prudential leadership. Schlesinger describes FDR's decision-making process as "inscrutable" (Schlesinger 1958, 528). Tugwell characterizes it as a system of "uncommon calculation" in which ends and means coalesced according to a mix that was unknown sometimes even to FDR himself (Tugwell 1957, 546). Perkins notes that "his intuitive understanding, his imagination, his moral and traditional bias, his sense of right and wrong—all entered into his mind and unless these flowed freely through his mind as he considered a subject, he was unlikely to come to any clear conclusion or ever to a clear understanding" (Perkins 1946, 21).

Like Washington, Lincoln, and Theodore Roosevelt before him, FDR took great risks as president and occasionally they backfired. It cannot be denied that sometimes these presidents schemed, plotted, and acted duplicitously. After initially seeking the counsel of the United States Senate in the formulation of foreign policy, Washington later tried his best to avoid all direct contact with that legislative body. Lincoln's immediate reaction to South Carolina's siege of Fort Sumter was a ruse pure and simple. TR was not above using cunning to outmaneuver Congress on matters relating to the conservation of natural resources. And FDR never was completely honest with the American people about the provocative nature of his destroyers-for-bases and lend-lease policies.

Such ploys are consistent with Aristotelian prudence only to the extent that they are a means of last resort, they serve just ends, and leaders never become smug or complacent about using them. Under these circumstances and within these strict limitations, schemes and plots in the hands of prudent presidents are examples of what Reinhold Niebuhr refers to as "love and power in tension" (Thompson 1956, 169).

Washington's, Lincoln's and the two Roosevelts' notable failures, discussed elsewhere in the book, demonstrate that they were flesh and blood human beings who hardly fit the conventional images of them as one-dimensional, wooden icons. But often, at defining moments in American history, such as World War II, their risks paid off. "There were indeed many times," historian Doris Kearns Goodwin writes, "when it seemed that (FDR) could see it all—the relationship of the home front to the war front; of the factories to the soldiers; of speeches to morale; of the government to the people; of war aims to the shape of the peace to come" (Goodwin 1994, 10).

As the noted author and presidential speech writer Archibald MacLeish remarks: "Let no man miss the point of Mr. Roosevelt's hold upon the minds of the citizens of the republic. . . . It is only to the free, inventive gestures of the human soul that men wholly and believingly respond" (MacLeish quoted in Schlesinger 1960, 192). These are precisely the qualities—the innate knowledge, penetrating vision, and open-mindedness in the face of catastrophic international events, and the strong moral beliefs combined with recognition of "what action permitted by (his beliefs) should, in the circumstances, be performed" (Oakeshott 1967, 168)—that link Franklin Delano Roosevelt's foreign policy to Aristotelian prudence.

Other distinct illustrations of prudent presidential leadership in American history are Thomas Jefferson's Louisiana Purchase in 1803, Harry Truman's adoption of the Marshall Plan in 1948, and Jimmy Carter's mediation of the Camp David peace accord between Israel and Egypt in 1978. In each of these instances the presidents involved took action that matched the requirements of Aristotelian prudence point for point: the desire to articulate and support noble ideals that serve the public interest; the capacity to determine a society's public interest by envisioning its present needs in the context of its past and future; the talent to propose laws and policies that accurately reflect their vision while dealing effectively with existing problems; and the skill to devise methods to overcome obstacles to the realization of proposed reforms that are consistent with their ideals.

On these occasions these presidents emphasized forever, but did not neglect today; relied on both transcendent ideals and contemporary political phenomena; recognized our capacity for good as well as our propensity for evil; balanced individual rights with moral responsiblities; and rejected relativistic and ideological approaches to the formulation of public policy. Fulfilling these criteria is never easily done, however. Throughout the course of American history presidents have generally adopted less complex leadership styles, as the following examples of idealistic presidential behavior illustrate.

CHAPTER 4

Idealistic Presidential Leadership

WOODROW WILSON AND THE TREATY OF VERSAILLES

When presidents provide prudent leadership they consciously refrain from asserting invulnerability in the face of the perplexing forces that comprise politics. They claim merely to have done the best they could under the circumstances. "I do the very best I know how, the very best I can, and I mean to keep doing so until the end," Lincoln once admitted during the Civil War. "If the end brings me out all right, what is said against me won't amount to anything. If the end brings me out wrong, ten angels swearing I was right would make no difference" (Lincoln quoted in Morgenthau 1966, 10). "I have no expectation of making a hit every time I come to bat," Franklin Delano Roosevelt confessed during the darkest days of World War II. "What I seek is the highest possible batting average not only for myself but for the team" (FDR quoted in Freidel 1990, 120).

When human beings lose such feelings of vulnerability and begin to think of themselves as limitless and self-sufficient, they step outside the realm of Aristotelian prudence and tend to become idealists. Jean-Jacques Rousseau articulates the characteristic conceit of the idealist when he argues that a political leader should feel "capable of changing human nature, so to speak . . . of altering man's constitution in order to strengthen it" (Rousseau 1978, 68). Woodrow Wilson displayed an attitude similar to

Rousseau's when he tried to get the United States to ratify the Treaty of Versailles at the end of World War I.

Wilson brought to the presidency in 1912 a belief in the superiority of American democracy and the conviction that he was destined to be an evangelist for its spread throughout the world. Against proponents of real-politik, he argued that foreign policy should be dictated by the democratic principles of trust, peace, and freedom. "There must be, not a balance of power, but a community of power," he said, "not organized rivalries, but an organized common peace" (Wilson quoted in Clements 1992, 163). Once in office Wilson attempted to put his ideas into action by agreeing to apologize to Colombia and pay it an indemnity for Theodore Roosevelt's ruthlessness in establishing the Panama Canal.

In Mexico and elsewhere, however, his theory of moral diplomacy quickly deteriorated into "moral imperialism" (106). For example, Wilson initially sought, through peaceful negotiations, to persuade the military dictator Victoriano Huerta that it was in the best interests of Mexico for him to voluntarily resign and permit a freely elected government to take his place. When, to nobody's surprise except perhaps Wilson's, Huerta refused, the president in 1914 sent the United States Navy and Marines to occupy the chief Mexican port of Veracruz. Later, in 1916, Wilson ordered 11,000 American troops under the command of General John Pershing to invade the northern part of the country. A similar chain of events occurred in Nicaragua, Haiti, and the Dominican Republic.

Wilson's experiences in Latin America demonstrate the conceit of all political idealists: their certainty that they alone know what is reasonable and morally correct for all humankind; their willingness to carry the torch and shoulder the burden of reason and morality for the entire world; and their serious underestimation of the proclivity for irrationality and evil in others as well as in themselves. In Latin America Wilson typically began by professing the need for a new, more humanistic foreign policy and wound up reverting to the same type of coercion that other, less self-righteous presidents had utilized there in the past. As French Premier Georges Clemenceau noted, Wilson "talked like Jesus Christ but acted like" a politician who does not bother to hide his or her self-serving motives (Clemenceau quoted in Blum 1956, 173).

After World War I started, but before the United States joined the fray, Wilson again exhibited a profound misunderstanding of political realities. In a reaffirmation of American neutrality, he insisted that Britain and Germany scrupulously observe the principles of traditional international law with regard to maritime trade. The problem was that these laws, which required naval vessels to warn unarmed merchant ships of an impending attack and to remove crews and passengers, could not be obeyed equally by both sides. The British, who hoped to persuade Wilson to abandon neutrality and to join their side, were using conventional warships to blockade goods exported by sea to Germany. But the Germans, whose only hope for victory depended on the United States remaining neutral and whose navy was no match for the English, put their trust in submarine warfare.

Since submarines rely on surprise attack and are too small to rescue many survivors, Wilson's plan of action ensured that it was only a matter of time before we would declare war on Germany. Unbeknownst to Wilson, and in authentic idealistic fashion, a policy he honestly considered to be evenhanded toward the belligerents and expertly constructed to preserve American neutrality as an ethical alternative to war wound up paving our way into the hostilities. If Wilson had consciously planned on joining the Allies in the first place, he at least could have begun to mobilize the economic and military resources necessary for rapid victory over a badly outnumbered foe. Instead the United States entered World War I in 1917 almost totally unprepared and thousands of innocent lives were unnecessarily lost on the battlefields of Europe.

From the outset Wilson made it clear that he considered the war to be a momentous crusade to end war and create a new world that would be safe for democracy. When hostilities subsided in 1918 he traveled to Versailles, France, with a wishlist of Fourteen Points he hoped would be incorporated into the final treaty. Included in his list were pleas for "peace without victory," an end to secret alliances, the fair disposition of colonial possessions, open use of the seas, armament reductions, free trade, the restoration of independence for Belgium, the creation of a Polish republic, the autonomy of several nationalities formerly subverted by the Austro-Hungarian and Ottoman empires, and the establishment of an international general assembly known as the League of Nations (Blum, Morgan, et al. 1977, 574).

Wilson fully expected stiff opposition from the other key Allied representatives. Clemenceau of France, David Lloyd George of Britain, Victorio Orlando of Italy, and Count Nobuaki Makino of Japan all subscribed to nationalistic power politics as an end in itself and were bent on making Germany pay dearly for the damage to their countries caused by the fighting. Wilson obviously disagreed with them but realized that the only way to achieve a satisfactory peace was through bargaining. On the other hand, he underestimated the force of nationalism in the United States and thus never really was prepared to negotiate as seriously with prominent American public officials, who found fault with the Fourteen Points, as he did with his counterparts at Versailles.

Wilson's shortsightedness, what biographer Arthur Walworth calls his "obtuseness to reality" (Walworth 1969, 219), proved fatal when, during the midterm congressional elections of 1918, Republicans gained sweeping majorities in both the Senate and House of Representatives. Standing to gain most from these results was Henry Cabot Lodge, Senate majority leader, chair of the influential Senate Foreign Relations Committee, and Wilson's archenemy. Lodge sought to discredit Wilson personally as well as for the direction he wanted to take the United States in world affairs and his unwillingness to share power with the Senate in the area of foreign policy. His specific point of contention involved the U.S. entrance into the League of Nations, which, Lodge felt, would interfere with American sovereignty. He was especially concerned about the portion of the League Covenant that read as follows:

> The Members of the League undertake to respect and preserve as against external aggression the territorial integrity and existing political independence of all Members of the League. In case of any such aggression or in case of any threat or danger of such aggression the Council shall advise upon the means by which this obligation shall be fulfilled. (Clements 1992, 192)

Since the number of senators who shared Lodge's reservations exceeded the one-third necessary to block ratification of treaties, Wilson found himself in a position where he would either have to compromise with his critics or face defeat. Although he was a professional political scientist, who had written extensively on the need for cooperation between the president and Congress in order to make American government work, Wilson chose not to budge. The crux of the Treaty of Versailles was the League, upon whose shoulders, he argued, rested the destiny of the world. Since, in his opinion, the success of the League depended on full American participation and total support, he concluded that any amendment of the treaty to allow greater independence for the United States would amount to a rejection of the entire peace process and rob humanity of what he claimed was its "only hope" for the future (Wilson quoted in Walworth 1969, 338).

When even his highly supportive wife, Edith, advised him to reach an accommodation with the Senate, Wilson replied: "Can't you see that I have no moral right to accept any change in a paper I have signed. . . . It is not *I* that will not accept; it is the nation's honor that is at stake. . . . Better a thousand times to go down fighting than to dip your colors to dishonorable compromise" (386). As Wilson earlier had boasted, "If I think (something) is right . . . I shall do so regardless of the circumstances" (187).

Unwilling to acknowledge failure or do what even his wife knew had to be done to achieve ratification, Wilson embarked on an exhausting whistle-stop tour across the United States designed to generate public support for his position. Over the course of 8,000 miles and thirty-seven speeches in September 1919 alone, he warned Americans that, if their representatives in Congress refused to accept the treaty as it was originally written, "within another generation there will be another world war" (Wilson quoted in Pious 1996, 59). Then, on September 25, in Pueblo, Colorado, Wilson collapsed and was taken back to the White House where he suffered a debilitating stroke.

Woodrow Wilson proved to be a better prophet than leader in this instance. The United States Senate never did ratify the Treaty of Versailles. Without American participation, the League of Nations became weak and ineffective. Twenty years to the month later, on September 1, 1939, Hitler invaded Poland and World War II began. Wilson deserves at least part of the blame for this tragic turn of events. His idealism blinded him to the realities of the American system of separation of powers and checks and balances—a system that, as a professional student of American politics, he should have known like the back of his hand. Wilson dug in his heels and repudiated compromise in a system that requires compromise between branches of government at every turn. Once he became convinced that the rules of American politics did not apply to him, that, in other words, he was invulnerable to the rules, the fate of the treaty and the League was sealed.

As a cynic Wilson would have willingly participated in the attempted plunder of Germany at Versailles. As a pragmatist he would have simply split the differences between his views and those of Lodge in an effort to gain the assent of the Senate. As a prudent leader he would have invited Lodge and other leading Senate Republicans to travel with him to France to participate in the peace proceedings. In this manner he would have given his most powerful American critics a stake in the formulation of the Versailles Treaty and prudently undercut their antagonistic attitude toward it. Wilson, however, found such a strategy to be unimaginable.

He apparently considered himself to be a Platonic philosopher king, for whom reality is composed solely of intangible universal ideals. By that standard his Fourteen Points are no doubt admirable. But the assumption that he could get Americans to accept them by the force of his will alone was nothing short of delusional. According to historian John Blum, the nobility Wilson "ascribed to his purposes precluded the tactical resilience without which the politics of persuasion could not work" (Blum 1956, 36). "It was inconceivable" to him, Arthur Walworth has written, "that responsible men could try to stop the process of inexorable universal law." In the end he refused to admit the possibility that the United States "would not put aside considerations of party and, acting as a principal, ratify the Covenant to which its accredited agent had committed it" (Walworth 1969, 359).

JOHN QUINCY ADAMS AND PATRONAGE

Since idealistic leaders refuse to acknowledge the less than wholesome aspects of politics, they typically are unable to deal with them effectively or use them to their advantage. The way John Quincy Adams mishandled patronage is characteristic of this self-defeating quality of idealistic political leadership. Patronage, or the spoils system as it is commonly called, plays an important role in the relationship between political parties and democracy in the United States. Parties perform certain functions that are essential to free government. As parties grow more cohesive they are able to execute these functions more effectively. By trading jobs for party cohesiveness, patronage thus helps to sustain American democracy.

The primary function of parties in the United States is to organize the struggle for political power. They recruit and nominate candidates for office, assist in the formulation of their platforms, campaign for them, and, in the event of defeat, act as the loyal opposition. The close attention paid by losing parties to the performance of incumbents serves to educate voters about salient political problems. The willingness of parties temporarily out of office to retain their loyalty to the American political system as a whole is preferable to the specter of frustrated factions advancing in military columns on presidential palaces. By seeking to gain the support of the majority, moreover, American political parties act to bring together voters from different racial, religious, ethnic, ideological, and socioeconomic groups. Without such consensus, a nation as diverse as the United States would be susceptible to the disunity that lurks below the surface of every democracy and poses a challenge to its existence.

In order for political parties to gain and maintain cohesion, it is necessary to develop a cadre of workers they can count on to get out the vote for their candidates. To maintain such a cadre, parties must reward them with government employment. As the heads of their parties, American presidents traditionally have used patronage to ensure their reelection and further their policy goals. Thomas Jefferson, Andrew Jackson, Abraham Lincoln and Franklin Roosevelt, among others, became legendary for their appointment of untold numbers of party loyalists to such positions as postmaster, collector of the port, Indian agent, United States attorney and assistant attorney, federal judge, and ambassador. Even Woodrow Wilson was persuaded to utilize patronage to gain support for his domestic reforms (Pious 1996, 168).

Political scientist Pendleton Herring has characterized patronage as "the tar baby of American politics" (Herring 1965, 349). We understand that patronage easily lends itself to corruption and inefficiency, but stick with it because we have not been able to come up with a suitable alternative. Such merit system laws as the 1883 Pendleton Act and the 1939 Hatch Act restrict patronage to a certain degree. However, its complete abolition would weaken political parties in the United States and make it increasingly difficult for them to locate nominees with sufficient majority appeal to win elections. Eventually powerful minority interests with single issue agendas would begin to take the place of traditional parties in the American political system, and further strain would be placed on our already precarious democratic consensus.

"Patronage is not an extraneous abuse," Herring writes. "Politicians have habitually taken their support where it was offered. The more they are cut off from patronage the more they are thrown for help upon the organizations in the community strong enough to provide dollars or votes or both" (366). According to political scientist V. O. Key:

> The truth is that we have contrived no system for the support of party that does not place considerable reliance on patronage. The party organization makes a democratic government work and charges a price for its services. Sometimes it becomes corrupt and levies an exorbitant charge. Fortunately not all political organizations are corrupt, and over the long run the spoils system has come to operate within narrower bounds. Yet until we invent some other system of political financing or new incentives for party service, the government, directly or indirectly, will contribute to the support of party activity. (Key 1967, 369)

These arguments seem to have been lost on John Quincy Adams. In 1824 he won one of the most complicated presidential elections in American history. There were four major candidates for president that year: William Crawford, secretary of the treasury under second-term incumbent James Monroe; Henry Clay, speaker of the United States House of Representatives; Andrew Jackson, the military hero of New Orleans during the War of 1812; and Adams, Monroe's secretary of state. Although Crawford was Monroe's favorite, Jackson led in the popular vote count. Since none of them polled a majority in the Electoral College, however, the election went to the House where each state delegation cast one vote from among the top three candidates. This eliminated Clay. When a serious illness sidelined Crawford, only Jackson and Adams were left in the running. In the House Clay threw the support of the states that had voted for him in the popular election behind Adams, who then emerged with the majority of votes necessary for victory.

Upon assuming office Adams appointed Clay secretary of state, a move that led to widespread charges of patronage abuse. Jackson called Clay "that Judas of the West" (Jackson quoted in Clark 1932, 233). Actually, nothing could be further from the truth. Adams despised the spoils system on principle and gave Clay the job primarily because he thought Clay was the one most qualified for it. Except for Clay, not a single member of Adams's cabinet had openly endorsed him for president (234). In fact many pro-Jackson politicians, including the controversial Postmaster General John McLean, served in the Adams administration. To Clay's suggestion that he remove an especially recalcitrant federal official, Adams replied:

> Should I remove this man for this cause, it must be upon some fixed principle, which would apply to others as well as to him. And where was it possible to draw the line? Of the customs house officers throughout the Union four-fifths, in all probability, were opposed to my election. They were all now in my power, and I had been urged very earnestly to sweep away my opponents and provide, with their places, for my friends. I can justify the refusal to adopt this policy only by the steadiness and consistency of my adhesion to my own. If I depart from this in one instance, I shall be called on by my friends to do the same in many. An insidious and inquisitional scrutiny into the personal dispositions of public officers will creep through the whole Union, and the most selfish and sordid passions will be kindled into activity to distort the conduct and misrepresent the feelings of men whose places may become the prize of slander upon them. (250–51)

The extent of Adams's opposition to patronage is illustrated by the General James Tallmadge affair. Tallmadge, the lieutenant governor of New York, played a crucial role in securing the state's presidential electors for Adams in 1824. In doing so he opposed New York's Jacksonian faction led by Martin Van Buren and De Witt Clinton, two of the most powerful figures in the state. Realizing that his future in New York politics had been compromised, Tallmadge asked Adams to appoint him to a post in the foreign service so that he could escape the country until the storm blew over. To Tallmadge's amazement and chagrin, Adams refused, claiming that he already had named another New Yorker, Rufus King, as minister to Britain and that it would not be fair for any state to "claim more than one overseas appointment" (Koenig 1996, 132). The irony was that King had supported Jackson in 1824 and was an ally of Van Buren and Clinton.

Had Adams adopted a cynical approach to patronage, he would have appointed only those people to federal positions who could offer him the most support without any regard for their job qualifications. Had he adopted a pragmatic approach, he would have traded jobs for favors with some regard for qualifications. Had he been a prudent leader on this issue, however, he would have appointed the most qualified people to federal positions who also could provide him with the monetary and political support necessary for him to be reelected.

Few presidents had as much political experience prior to occupying the White House as John Quincy Adams. He literally grew up in American politics as the son of John Adams, one of our Founding Fathers and the second President of the United States. He was a U.S. senator from Massachusetts and served as Ambassador to Holland, Russia, and Britain. As Monroe's secretary of state, he played a critical role in formulating the Monroe Doctrine.

Despite this extensive experience, Adams never was able to come to terms with the realities of American party politics. Disregarding the advice of colleagues, he contributed to the failure of his administration by displaying the "political ineptness" of a novice (Nagel 1997, 419) on the subject of patronage. To no one's surprise, after 1824 Adams's Democratic-Republican party faded away. His presidency became "a tragic episode" in American history (Blum, Morgan, et al. 1977, 208). In 1828 he lost to Jackson by a wide margin of electoral votes.

JIMMY CARTER AND THE MARIEL BOAT LIFT

Jimmy Carter's foreign policy toward Cuba, resulting in the Mariel boat lift that proved to be embarrassing to the United States in 1980, represents the folly of political idealism in vivid detail. Carter made the critical idealistic mistake of assuming that morality applies to nations and individuals in exactly the same way. For example, it is possible to imagine circumstances under which it would be fitting for individuals to risk death in the name of abstract moral principles. There would be no United States today, as a matter of fact, unless Americans 200 years ago were prepared to fight and die for the ideals of freedom and independence. On the other hand, it would be imprudent for political leaders to sacrifice the future of their countries and the lives of their fellow citizens for the sake of an abstraction alone. We mock the legend of the ancient ruler who refused to defend his civilization against an invasion that occurred during a monsoon because his religion prohibited fighting in the rain.

As the world's most powerful democracy, it is morally necessary for the United States to be concerned about the fate of human rights around the globe. But it also is morally necessary for the United States to worry about its own interests, both for Americans themselves and so that, from a position of strength, the country can continue to exert pressure on undemocratic regimes to reform. How to balance the priorities of national self-interest and human rights is a question only prudent negotiators exercising all the discretion at their disposal can answer, looking at one situation and one country at a time.

Of course, relations between the United States and Cuba were unsound long before Carter came into office. After the Spanish-American War in 1898 the United States made Cuba a protectorate and imposed on it the harsh conditions of the Platt Amendment, which permitted American forces to occupy the country and establish a naval base on Guantanamo Bay. The protectorate ended in 1902, only to be replaced by a treaty that gave the United States the right to intervene in Cuban affairs in the event of a foreign threat or domestic unrest. In 1906 President Theodore Roosevelt exercised that right by landing American troops again in Cuba where they remained for three years.

The United States occupied Cuba twice more in the twentieth century in order to protect the sizable American investments that had developed there. By the end of World War II, Americans owned 80 percent of Cuba's utilities, 40 percent of its sugar, and 90 percent of its mineral wealth (Ambrose 1993, 167). Acting as a front man for these interests, as well as for the Mafia with its headquarters in Havana, was the military dictator Fulgencio Batista. In 1959 a band of guerrillas led by Fidel Castro overthrew Batista. When Castro proceeded to nationalize American companies without compensating them, establish a dictatorial regime of his own, and espouse a Communist ideology, President Dwight Eisenhower granted the Central Intelligence Agency permission to train approximately 1,400 Cuban exiles for an invasion that was supposed to take place with enough American military support to ensure success.

The final decision to invade was left for incoming President John F. Kennedy to make, which he did in April 1961. The kind of leadership Kennedy provided during what became known as the Bay of Pigs incident is discussed in chapter 6. For the moment it is only necessary to remark that the invasion was a complete failure: It caused the Cuban Missile crisis of 1962 that brought the world within a hair's breadth of nuclear catastrophe; and it precipitated a severe American economic boycott of Cuba that still exists. Through all this, Castro remained relatively unfazed and determined to maintain the totalitarian nature of his regime.

During the ensuing decades, indeed, Castro embarked on a crusade to export his brand of Communist revolution and dictatorship throughout Latin America and Africa. Cuban military advisors and/or troops reportedly were sent to aid rebels opposing regimes backed by the United States in such countries as Bolivia, El Salvador, Grenada, Nicaragua, Algeria, Angola, the Congo (Zaire), Somalia, and Ethiopia. This, then, was the legacy of distrust and hostility between the United States and Cuba that Jimmy Carter inherited when he became president in 1976.

Carter considered human rights to be the fundamental basis of his foreign policy. As he said in his inaugural address, "Our commitment to human rights must be absolute" (Carter 1982, 20). With regard to Cuba, and consistent with what was supposed to be his new emphasis on peace and good will, Carter offered Castro the olive branch. He cancelled reconnaissance overflights, discontinued the ban on travel to Cuba by Americans, allowed Cuban boats to fish in U.S. territorial waters, and established a mechanism by which the two countries would renew diplomatic relations and enforce mutual anti-hijacking procedures (Smith 1987, 102). It was anticipated that Cuba would reciprocate by instituting significant democratic reforms. But Carter's expectations were unrealistic, since Castro agreed to free only some political prisoners and make immigration to the United States less burdensome for some Cubans.

Additional problems arose when the Cuban-American community took Carter's human rights foreign policy objectives one step further and began to urge opponents of Castro to hijack Cuban vessels to take them to Miami. Castro reacted with a vengeance to what he interpreted as a direct violation of the anti-hijacking agreement that the United States and Cuba had just reached and as another example of American interference with Cuban internal affairs. On April 18, 1980, he publicly announced that all Cubans, dissatisfied with democratic conditions in their homeland, were free to leave from the port of Mariel on boats supplied for that express purpose by Cuban exiles living in the United States. By May thousands of these boats had appeared at the port (213). At first the passengers were Cubans with family ties to the exiles. But their status soon changed when Castro began loading the boats with several thousand criminals and mental patients (214).

Upon their arrival in Miami, the situation turned from bad to worse. Many of the immigrants camped out on the streets of the city. The misfits eventually were sent to federal prisons and county jails where some 1,750 of them remain to this day. Certain elements in the local African-American community felt shortchanged by all the attention paid by government officials to the plight of the immigrants. Aroused partly by their feelings of neglect, these elements staged the worst race riot in the history of Miami in the summer of 1980.

How could Carter allow Castro to play him for such a fool and make such a mockery of American foreign policy? Apparently Carter's idealism blinded him to the reality that his emphasis on human rights would only be able to influence foreign leaders who were friendly to the United States and/or depended heavily on American aid. Carter's objectives thus enjoyed noteworthy successes in the Middle East with President Anwar Sadat of Egypt and Prime Minister Menachem Begin of Israel and in Panama with General Omar Torrijos. In Iran he was able to convince a reluctant shah to belatedly relax his tyrannic rule. However, for other leaders such as Russian Premier Leonid Brezhnev and the Ayatollah Khomeini, who deposed the shah in Iran, Carter's pleas fell on deaf ears. In the Soviet Union Carter's human rights policy was one of the factors that led to the demise of the SALT II treaty for the reduction of nuclear armaments. In Iran his policy contributed to the replacement of one tyrant, who happened to be our ally, with an equally despotic one who became one of our most intractable enemies. Ironically it was Khomeini's capture of the U.S. embassy in Teheran, where fifty-three Americans were held hostage for over a year, that helped convince voters to substitute Ronald Reagan for Carter during the 1980 presidential election.

Carter's folly was that, by pledging the unconditional determination of the United States to protect civil liberties everywhere and at any time, he deprived American diplomats of the discretion necessary for them to be effective negotiators. On the specific question of U.S.-Cuban relations, Carter seems to have ruled out pragmatism and mistakenly assumed that foreign policy choices were limited to either realpolitik, which cynically denies the influence of ideals, or idealism, which completely ignores the impulses that cause nations to pursue their selfish interests. Actually, there is a prudent alternative available to political leaders who possess the imagination and ingenuity necessary to reconcile ideals with national interests. Reaching such reconciliations may be difficult to accomplish, but it is not impossible. Political scientist Robert Osgood discusses the possibility:

> Although it is morally imperative that men should not minimize the contradictions between national self-interest and universal ideals, it is equally imperative that they should not exaggerate the contradictions by positing a rigid antithesis between these two ends. The utopians, anxious to assert the claims of idealism and impatient with reality, or the Realist, exasperated by the inability of utopians to perceive the reality of national egoism, may be tempted to simplify the troublesome moral dilemma of international society by declaring that ideals and self-interest are mutually exclusive or that one end is the only valid standard of international conduct. But neither view does much to illuminate reality or advance the cause of idealism. In very few situations are statesmen faced with a clear choice between ideals and national self-interest; in almost all situations they are faced with the task of reconciling the two. If they succeed in reconciling them so

as to maximize ideal values, they will come as near to moral perfection as anyone can reasonably hope. (Osgood 1965, 22–23)

Taking his cue from Aristotle, who distinguished between theoretical and practical reason, Edmund Burke observed the tragic results of attempts by French *philosophes* to apply unreconstructed ideals to a society historically unprepared for them. As Burke predicted, the hopes and dreams of the radicals went unrealized and a society was created that turned out to be more repressive than the one they meant to change. Had his foreign policy been informed by the principles of Aristotelian prudence, perhaps Carter could have developed a greater appreciation for the difficulties involved in bringing human rights to Castro's Cuba. Perhaps he could have more effectively offered at least the possibility of easing the embargo on Cuban trade with the United States in return for some relaxation of Cuban totalitarianism. And perhaps he could have found a way to avoid the embarrassment to his presidency of the Mariel boat lift.

BILL CLINTON'S HEALTH CARE INITIATIVE

The defeat of Bill Clinton's health care initiative in 1994 was due primarily to his inability to reconcile the ideals of universal health care with the realities of American interest group politics. Ironically, Clinton's idealism in this instance had little to do with the substance of his proposed reforms, which were conventionally market driven, but rather with the process he chose to pursue them.

When the framers of the Constitution created the foundation for American pluralism in 1788 their greatest fear was that factions would interfere with the possibility of achieving political justice in the United States. In *Federalist #10* James Madison observed that, since the desire to serve ourselves is a fixed element of human nature, the most pressing function of American government must be to discover a means by which to transform our selfish instincts into the public interest. "The inference to which we are brought," Madison wrote, "is that the *causes* of faction cannot be removed and that relief is only to be sought in the means of controlling its effects" (Madison, Hamilton, and Jay 1961, 80).

The method we have chosen to bring about this transformation involves the adoption of such constitutional principles as federalism, separation of powers, and checks and balances whose explicit purpose is to fragment government and cause it to develop a deliberate, incremental style of operation. By slowing down and debilitating the American political system in this fashion, we have sought to enhance individual initiative and promote competition between groups organized by private citizens to pressure government on their behalf. Our conscious strategy thus has been to control factionalism by fostering it with the expectation that the public interest of the United States eventually will emerge as competing American selfish interests serve to cancel each other out. As Madison maintained in *Federalist #51*, "ambition must be made to counteract ambition" (Madison, Hamilton, and Jay 1961, 322).

It was the intention of the framers that laws passed and policies implemented by this pluralist system would represent a consensus of the interests most directly influenced by them. Conversely, attempts to pass laws and implement policies that do not reflect the interests of influential groups would be doomed to failure. Herein lies the source of the miscalculations that led to the defeat of Clinton's health care reforms.

There clearly is a need for health care reform in the United States. Most workers in this country receive health insurance through their jobs. Medicare and Medicaid cover the elderly, the extremely poor, and the disabled. Veterans' hospitals care for former members of the armed services. Yet over 15 percent of Americans have no health insurance at all. An additional 72,000,000 lack coverage for the spiralling cost of prescription drugs (Johnson and Broder 1996, 62). Thirteen percent constitute the working poor whose employers do not provide health insurance and who make too much money to qualify for Medicaid. This segment of the population typically goes to hospital emergency rooms when their conditions reach the critical stage and the cost of treating them becomes prohibitive (Burns, Peltason, et al. 1998, 540).

Those who have health care coverage may find that when they change jobs their preexisting medical conditions are no longer insured. Health management organizations (HMOs) often deny patients the referrals necessary for treatment by specialists and impose unreasonable time limits on hospital stays for certain procedures such as childbirth. Moreover, some employers remove coverage for retirees whose lifelong savings are depleted when they become hospitalized for a catastrophic illness or a sickness related to old age (Johnson and Broder 1996, 382).

Previous attempts by presidents to rectify these inequities aroused fear on the part of individuals that big government and bureaucratic red tape would deprive them of free choice among doctors, hospitals, and health plans and provoked antagonism from interest groups that benefited most from the status quo. The view expressed frequently by middle-class Americans with health care provided by their employers has been that they favor universal coverage as long as someone else pays for it. It was these pressures that kept FDR from including compulsory national health insurance in his Social Security Act of 1935 and that derailed Harry Truman's plans for universal health care in 1948. When Congress, with the support of the Reagan administration, enacted the Catastrophic Coverage Act of 1988 and decided to finance it with higher Medicare premiums, the reaction from senior citizens was so adverse that the law was soon repealed (Burns, Peltason, et al. 1998, 537).

Compared to the governments of Canada, Germany, Japan, the Netherlands, and Great Britain, which subsidize approximately 75 percent of the total health care costs in their countries, the American government only pays 46 percent of the costs. To make matters worse, the price of American health care is the most expensive in the world. For example, in Germany, where Chancellor Otto von Bismarck mandated government health insurance in 1883, health care expenditures amounted to 8.6 percent of the 1996 country's gross domestic product (GDP). During that same year health care costs in the United States constituted 14.2 percent of our own GDP (544). Over the last decade, indeed, the amount Americans paid for medical treatment increased by a rate more than double the rise in our cost of living (Thobaben, Schlagheck, and Funderburk 1998, 45). The reaction of government and private industry to these escalating charges has been to reduce insurance benefits while increasing the share of health costs paid by employees.

Against this backdrop the Clinton administration initiated its version of health care reform in 1992. Although they turned out to be "far too complex" (Drew 1994, 193) and attempted "to do far too much far too quickly" (304), the reforms Clinton had in mind actually were quite moderate in scope because they continued to emphasize free enterprise and the private realm. His proposed Health Security Act required employers to provide 80 percent of comprehensive health insurance for their workers, including preventive care and prescription drugs. The self-employed and unemployed would pay a share of the cost of their coverage, based on how much they earned. It would have been up to the national government to pick up the rest of the tab in part by increasing taxes on tobacco products.

In order to contain costs, large purchasing groups of employers and consumers, called alliances, would have been created to bargain with privately owned HMOs for medical care at competitive prices. Drug companies would have been prohibited from raising their prices higher than the rate of inflation and were to be given tax breaks if they spent more money on research and development than on advertising. Clinton's goal was to have the Health Security Act passed by Congress during the first hundred days of his administration and universal coverage financed mostly by employer mandates implemented shortly thereafter.

The Health Security Act itself was a product of the Presidential Task Force on National Health Reform that Clinton had appointed with his wife as chair. From the outset the task force provoked controversy by employing immoderate methods that violated the norms of consensual politics to implement Clinton's essentially moderate goals. Although all of its appointees were highly intelligent and obviously devoted to the cause, many of them had no or limited previous experience with the give and take expected of knowledgeable participants in the American governmental process. When they chose to meet secretly, other more politically seasoned supporters of health care reform got the impression that their input was not welcomed. When they omitted Republicans from their ranks, the hearts of GOP opponents were further hardened against reform. When they presented the act to Congress as a *fait accompli*, influential Democrats in the House and Senate were deprived of an opportunity to reach agreement with the task force through bargaining and negotiation.

When they refused to budge on employer mandates, small business groups reacted by spending in excess of $50 million on a negative advertising campaign that featured television spots in which two actors portraying a middle-class white couple named "Harry and Louise" outlined what small businessmen and women found most objectionable about the act (Johnson and Broder 1996, 212). Ironically many large businesses, including General Motors, Ford, Chrysler, and U.S. West, favored Clinton's plan because they were already subsidizing more than 80 percent of their employees' health care benefits.

Acting as a lightning rod for the criticism was Hillary Rodham Clinton. Those who stood to lose by any change in the health care status quo often went beyond assailing the logic of the Health Security Act to engage in vicious ad hominem attacks on her character. Anti-feminists assaulted her for being too independent and outspoken. Some feminists faulted her for riding on her husband's coattails and not being independent enough. Others resented someone, for whom they did not vote and with whom they disagreed, exerting so much political power.

Through it all President Clinton adopted the typical idealistic strategy of absolutely refusing to compromise. According to Lawrence O'Donnell, former chief of staff of the Senate Finance Committee, Clinton and his advisors seemed to be on a "religious crusade" (266). As Clinton told Congress during his 1994 state of the union address: "If you send me legislation that does not guarantee every American private health insurance that can never be taken away . . . you will force me to take this pen . . . veto the legislation, and we'll come right back here and start all over again" (267). In typical idealistic fashion, it never occurred to him that a plan he considered morally and logically unquestionable would be rejected by the American people. As he later admitted to journalists Haynes Johnson and David Broder, he believed his health care reforms would prevail "because I thought the need to do something was so self-evident" (198).

By 1994, however, the Health Security Act was soundly defeated, never even coming to a vote in Congress. Instead of playing the incremental game of American consensual politics, outlined by Madison in *The Federalist Papers*, Clinton's efforts to institute changes in the health care system of the United States on his own terms virtually overnight had the reverse effect of turning Americans off to further government control over their lives. In the midterm elections of 1994, they voted to turn back the clock on FDR's New Deal policy outlook. Thanks in part to Clinton's idealistic approach to health care, decades of Democratic control of Congress had come to at least a temporary halt.

If Clinton had applied a prudential strategy to the issue of health care, he would have simplified his proposed changes to make them easier for the American public to appreciate, done more to court small business groups by lowering employer mandates, taken the guidance of senior congressional Democrats more seriously, and appointed someone other than his wife to head the reform effort. If he had acted cynically, he would have not been willing to risk his own power by seeking to create a less unjust health care system for what amounts to a minority of people in the United States. As a pragmatist, he would have been satisfied with more modest changes, such as increased coverage for the indigent and elderly through Medicaid and Medicare.

Yet, like John Quincy Adams, Wilson, and Carter before him, the story of Clinton and health care is one of a morally defensible ideal defended in a politically indefensible manner. The same may be said of Andrew Johnson's willingness to risk impeachment in order to return the United States to normalcy after the Civil War. In theory there is nothing wrong with giving government jobs to the most qualified applicants, seeking to reunite a country torn apart by civil war, working to sustain peace between nations, supporting human rights, and aiming to provide quality medical treatment for every American. In practice there are serious political impediments to achieving such ideals that must not be underestimated if presidents want to maximize their chances for success. When John Quincy Adams, Andrew Johnson, Wilson, Carter, and Clinton adopted a sense of naive invulnerability toward these impediments, the fate of their endeavors was sealed.

CHAPTER 5

Cynical Presidential Leadership

RICHARD NIXON AND WATERGATE

Compared to idealists who ignore material circumstances in favor of moral goals, cynics abandon moral goals altogether. Whereas idealists practice eternal optimism, cynics are pessimistic to the core. Compared to idealists who profess to care about humankind, cynics worry only about themselves. Whereas idealists can be arrogantly self-righteous, cynics are outright scoundrels. Niccolo Machiavelli spoke for all cynics when he counseled a leader not to "keep his word when to do so would go against his interest, or when the reasons that made him pledge it no longer apply. Doubtless if all men were good, this rule would be bad; but since they are a sad lot, and keep no faith with you, you in your turn are under no obligation to keep it with them" (Machiavelli 1992, 48). Richard Nixon seems to have followed Machiavelli's advice when he behaved cynically and acted like a scoundrel during the Watergate crisis.

The arrest of five men on June 17, 1972, for breaking into the Democratic National Committee headquarters located at the Watergate office and hotel complex in Washington, D.C., set into motion a two-year chronology of events that eventually led Richard Nixon to become the only president to resign in American history. The burglars were caught in the act of repairing bugging devices on the telephones of Lawrence O'Brien, head of the Demo-

cratic National Committee, that they originally had installed during a previous break-in two weeks earlier. When apprehended, the men were found
to have fifty-three sequentially numbered $100 bills in their possession. A
year before, essentially this same group had broken into the office of the
psychiatrist treating Daniel Ellsberg, searching for information that could
be used to discredit Ellsberg for leaking the classified "Pentagon Papers" to
the American press (Ambrose 1989, 2: 558).

What was the link between the burglars and Nixon? All of them were on
the payroll of Nixon's campaign organization, the Committee to Re-elect
the President (CREEP). Their leader was James McCord, chief of security
for CREEP. McCord's supervisor was G. Gordon Liddy, counsel to CREEP,
who in turn worked with E. Howard Hunt, a former CIA agent hired as a
presidential consultant. Scholars speculate that John Mitchell, former attorney general and former director of CREEP, had given Hunt $200,000 in ille-
gal campaign contributions to organize break-ins like the ones that occurred at the office of Ellsberg's psychiatrist and at Watergate. Known as
the "plumbers" in the White House, Hunt's group was supposed to locate
and plug the sources of leaks of sensitive presidential material (Pious 1996,
96). Mitchell's point man in this operation was Jeb Stuart Magruder, who
hired Liddy, Hunt, and McCord on the advice of Charles Colson, another
presidential staffer. Colson claimed to be acting in response to Nixon's direct orders to counteract the leaks by any means, including illegal ones if
necessary. "I don't give a damn how it's done," Colson said Nixon told him.
"Do whatever has to be done. . . . I don't want to be told why it can't be done.
I want the most complete investigation that can be conducted. . . . I don't
want excuses. I want results. I want it done; whatever the cost" (Colson
quoted in Ambrose 1989, 2: 450).

Exactly what were McCord and his associates doing in Lawrence
O'Brien's office? In 1972 Nixon was trailing Democratic presidential hope-
ful Edmund Muskie in the polls and Nixon presumably ordered the burglars to uncover whatever strategies the Democrats had in store for the
upcoming election. But another, much more sinister, motive may have been
involved. O'Brien once worked for the reclusive multibillionaire Howard
Hughes. It has been alleged that Nixon also wanted to find out what
O'Brien knew about money reportedly given by Hughes to Nixon and his
brother Donald in return for favorable antitrust decisions (Barber 1992, 156).

Whether Nixon ever specifically ordered the "plumbers" to bug
O'Brien's telephones is not clear. We do know, however, that Nixon was responsible for creating an atmosphere of paranoia, hatefulness, and cynicism in the Oval Office that could very well have led to such behavior.
Hugh Scott, the Republican Senate minority leader at the time and nor-

mally a Nixon loyalist, described that atmosphere as "deplorable, disgusting, shabby and immoral" (Scott quoted in White 1975, 297). We also know, from transcripts of conversations with aides that Nixon secretly taped, that once the Watergate arrests were made he participated in an overt, full-fledged coverup of the burglaries and his connection to them.

On June 19 Nixon had his press secretary, Ron Ziegler, dismiss reports of presidential involvement in the Watergate break-in with the now infamous words, "I'm not going to comment from the White House on a third-rate burglary attempt" (Ziegler quoted in Schell 1975, 265). Nixon paid the burglars hush money to guarantee their silence. While serving as a go-between for the bribes, Hunt's wife was killed in a 1972 plane crash. Ten thousand dollars in $100 bills were found in her purse (Dickinson 1974, 1: 40). On the pretext of national security, Nixon tried to use the CIA to interfere with FBI investigations of the break-in and coverup. He refused to give either the Senate Watergate Committee or Archibald Cox, the special prosecutor for the executive branch probe of the Watergate affair, access to the tapes. When Cox sought a court order for them, Nixon precipitated the "Saturday Night Massacre" of October 20, 1973, by firing Cox and causing the resignations of Attorney General Elliot Richardson and Deputy Attorney General William Ruckelshaus.

Of particular interest to Cox and his successor, Leon Jaworski, were nine tapes of Nixon talking about Watergate with Mitchell, chief of staff H. R. Haldeman, senior White House aide John Erlichman, and White House Counsel John Dean. Nixon claimed that the historic presidential power of executive privilege allowed him to maintain the confidentiality of these discussions. Although in *U.S. v. Nixon* the Supreme Court unanimously rejected his arguments, some of the material he finally turned over to Jaworski contained significant gaps and erasures. A final tape, released after the House of Representatives Judiciary Committee voted 27 to 11 to approve an article of impeachment against him, revealed what became known as the "smoking gun"—Nixon ordering Haldeman to tell the FBI, "Don't go any further into this case, period" (Nixon quoted in Barber 1992, 159).

By this time even the archconservative senator Barry Goldwater had had enough. "You can only be lied to so often," Goldwater was quoted as saying, "and it's time to take a stand that we want out" (Goldwater quoted in Nixon 1978, 1069). James St. Clair, head of the Watergate legal defense team, felt compromised by Nixon's duplicity and feared that he could be indicted for his unwitting participation in the cover-up (1055). Lacking sufficient support in Congress to avoid being removed from office, Nixon resigned on August 9, 1974, and Vice President Gerald Ford took his place. In September Ford pardoned the former president for any federal crimes he may have committed.

Did the sytem work? Was Nixon's decision to step down a validation of American politics? To the extent that equal justice under the law is considered to be one of our most cherished principles, Watergate was nothing short of a disaster. The final bill of impeachment issued by the House against Nixon included charges of obstructing justice, using the Internal Revenue Service to harass political foes, planting illegal wiretaps, and refusing to comply with subpoenas. He also cheated on his federal income tax returns to the tune of half a million dollars and availed himself of millions of dollars of federal funds to improve his private residences in San Clemente, California, and Key Biscayne, Florida (Blum, Morgan, et al. 1977, 811). Suffice it to say that if Americans other than the president were accused of such crimes, they would hardly be permitted to walk away from them scot-free.

Watergate also represents a serious challenge to the basic faith Americans must have in their democratic government if American democracy is to survive and prosper. As students of political socialization point out, presidents symbolize the political system for most citizens. The president usually is the first public official of whom we are aware (Greenstein 1974, 154). To the extent that we develop a positive view of presidential performance, we tend to have a positive view of American government as a whole. Since this socialization process begins at an early age, our perception of how presidents perform while we are growing up can influence our conclusions about politics for the rest of our lives. Herein lies Nixon's Watergate legacy: he may very well have taught a whole generation of Americans that their government cannot be trusted.

Nixon never stopped proclaiming his innocence. From Disneyworld in late 1973 he intoned, "I am not a crook" (Bernstein and Woodward 1974, 334). Later, in his *Memoirs*, he insisted that Watergate was nothing more than "an annoying and strictly political problem" (Nixon 1978, 646). What did he consider his biggest mistake in the whole affair? Not being calculating enough to destroy the tapes, he wrote (1004). What did he have to say about the criminal activities to which he admitted being associated—the wiretaps, interference with the FBI, misuse of the IRS, and so forth? Equating his own behavior during the Vietnam War era to Lincoln's efforts to maintain the integrity of the United States, he explained to television commentator David Frost in a widely publicized 1977 interview: "Well, when the President does it that means that it is not illegal" (Nixon quoted in Ambrose 1989, 2: 662). In the final analysis, it was this completely oblivious attitude toward the moral implications of his actions that marks Watergate as the most cynical example of presidential behavior in American history.

To historian Stephen Ambrose, Nixon "was the ultimate cynic, a President without principle in domestic politics" (Ambrose 1989, 10). To Arthur Schlesinger, Nixon and his crowd were unscrupulous people "who had been led to understand that the Presidency was above the law and that the end justified the means" (Schlesinger 1973, 268). To publisher William Randolph Hearst, Jr., he was "a man totally immersed in the cheapest and sleaziest kind of conniving" (Hearst quoted in Barber 1992, 158). To George McGovern, who lost to Nixon in the lopsided 1972 presidential election, he created "both a moral and a Constitutional crisis of unprecedented dimensions" (157). Perhaps Theodore White, author of the popular *Making of the President* series, articulated the point most eloquently:

> The true crime of Richard Nixon was simple: he destroyed the myth that binds America together, and for this he was driven from power.
>
> The myth he broke was critical—that somewhere in American life there is at least one man who stands for law, the President. That faith surmounts all daily cynicism, all evidence or suspicion of wrongdoing by lesser leaders, all corruptions, all vulgarities, all the ugly compromises of daily striving and ambition. That faith holds that all men are equal before the law and protected by it; and that no matter how the faith may be betrayed elsewhere, at one particular point—the Presidency—justice will be done beyond prejudice, beyond rancor, beyond the possibility of a fix. It was that faith that Richard Nixon broke, betraying those who voted for him even more than those who voted against him. (White 1975, 322)

THOMAS JEFFERSON AND THE TRIAL OF AARON BURR

Nixon's blatant disregard for the rule of law was in direct violation of the ideals set forth by Thomas Jefferson and the other American founders. In 1807, ironically, Jefferson violated the ideal of the rule of law himself during the trial for treason of his former vice president, Aaron Burr. Jefferson's relentless pursuit of Burr's guilt, contrary to the facts of the case, is another distinct illustration of cynical presidential behavior.

Rarely has American history known a more curious figure than Aaron Burr. He was the son of one of the founders of Princeton University. His mother was the daughter of the talented theologian Jonathan Edwards. During the Revolutionary War he rose to the rank of colonel and served on the staffs of George Washington and Benedict Arnold. Afterward he became active in New York politics, defeating Alexander Hamilton's father-in-law for a seat in the United States Senate. In 1800 he was placed on the presidential ballot with Jefferson in order to secure New York's electoral votes for the Democratic-Republican party. When Jefferson and Burr unexpectedly tied with seventy-three electoral votes apiece, the election was thrown into the House of Representatives. There, aided by Hamilton, Jefferson eventually emerged victorious and Burr was relegated to the vice-presidency.

Since Jefferson was convinced that Burr had cheated him by making secret deals for votes in the House, he refused to cooperate with his vice president and left Burr to lanquish in office. With the support of dissident Federalists, who considered uniting New York and New England into a separate confederacy that would secede from the Union, Burr ran for governor of New York in 1804. When opposition from Hamilton again led to his defeat, the volatile Burr killed him in a duel on July 11, 1804. It was while Burr was a fugitive from the law in New York and New Jersey that he engaged in certain activities that led to his being arrested, charged, and tried for treason in 1807.

Exactly what Burr had in mind and planned to do remain in doubt to this day. Rumor had it that Burr, realizing his career in government had ended, wished to exploit the dissatisfaction of the agricultural Western territories with a political system they perceived to be controlled by Eastern business interests. Toward that end, he supposedly sought to enlist the aid of the British to separate the West from the Union and organize it into a vast new empire with New Orleans as its capital and himself as its head. Another rumor was that he wanted to invade Mexico, conquer it, and crown himself king. His co-conspirators in these intrigues were said to be James Wilkinson, the commanding general of the United States Army, who happened to be a spy working for the government of Spain, and Harman Blennerhassett, a wealthy speculator living on an island in the Ohio River.

Whatever Burr's plans might have been, they were squelched when Wilkinson, seeking to gain favor with the administration and repay his Spanish masters, sold him out to Jefferson. In a letter written on October 21, 1806, Wilkinson warned the president that Burr was preparing to descend upon New Orleans with a force of approximately 1,000 men supported by the British navy (Abernathy 1968, 189). On Jefferson's orders Burr was arrested and taken to Richmond, Virginia, along with Blennerhassett to be tried under the supervision of the chief justice of the United States Supreme Court, John Marshall. Richmond became the site of Burr's trial because the federal circuit court that had jurisdiction over Blennerhassett's island on the Ohio River was located there. Marshall presided because he was the principal judge of the Richmond federal circuit. Allowing Marshall to preside over this case was a decision Jefferson soon would regret.

Jefferson was a supremely paradoxical figure in his own right. He advocated a theory of natural rights and was the author of the statement, "We hold these truths to be self-evident, that all men are created equal," but owned slaves and considered them to be inferior to whites. He believed in decentralizing American government, but was one of our most powerful presidents. He taught the benefits of agrarian values over industrial ones, but operated a very successful nail factory. He insisted on balancing the federal budget, but amassed a $15 million public debt by purchasing the Louisiana territory. Historian Joseph Ellis calls Jefferson the "American Sphinx" and describes him as "a series of disjointed personalities" (Ellis 1997, 13). In the words of the noted Jefferson biographer Merrill Peterson, he simply was "an impenetrable man" (Peterson 1970, viii). According to political scientist Leonard Levy, he was a dedicated civil libertarian who also had a darker, more devious side to his personality. Jefferson was in the habit of "talking one way and acting another," Levy writes (Levy 1963, x). As it turned out, unfortunately, in the Burr trial he talked and acted like a cynic.

The ensuing hearings "attracted as much attention as any trial that was ever held in the United States" (Abernathy 1968, 244). The cast of political heavyweights participating in it included Marshall, Luther Martin, the renowned attorney who served as Burr's defense counsel, John Randolph, the influential states' rights advocate chosen as foreman of the grand jury, and Andrew Jackson, who testified on Burr's behalf. George Hay, U.S. Attorney for the Virginia District and a son-in-law of James Monroe, charged Burr with a "misdemeanor for having set on foot an expedition against the dominions of the King of Spain" and with "treason for having assembled an armed force for the purpose of seizing the city of New Orleans, revolutionizing Orleans Territory, and separating the Western from the Atlantic states" (230).

Marshall handed down his instructions to the jury on the last day of August. Pointing to Article III Section 3 of the Constitution, the chief justice ruled that treason consists of an overt act of "levying war" against the United States or of overtly "adhering to their enemies, giving them aid and comfort." It is insufficient to merely intend to commit treason, he argued, and there must be at least "two witnesses to the same overt act." The jury took only twenty-five minutes to find Burr innocent. In their opinion the government had not met the burden of these stringent constitutional requirements.

Jefferson's behavior before, during, and after the trial verged on hysteria. He tried to prejudice the proceedings through repeated public pronouncements of Burr's guilt. He maintained far and wide that there is in fact no significant difference between intending to commit treason and actually committing it. He accused Marshall of participating in a Federalist party plot against him. He urged the passage of a bill "suspending the writ of habeas corpus for three months in all cases of persons charged with treason or other high crimes against the United States and arrested or imprisoned on authority of the President or anyone acting under his direction" (Levy 1963, 86). He sought to interfere with the historic independence of the judiciary by proposing a constitutional amendment that would permit the president and Congress to remove federal judges if they disagreed with their decisions. "The nation will judge both the offender and judges for themselves," he wrote. "If a member of the Executive or Legislature does wrong, the day is never far distant when the people will remove him. They will then see and amend the error in our Constitution which makes any branch independent of the rest" (Jefferson quoted in Beloff 1965, 176).

The verdict, he said, was "equivalent to a proclamation of impunity to every traitorous combination which may be formed to destroy the Union" (Jefferson quoted in Peterson 1970, 872). Jefferson rationalized his cynical conduct by equating the Burr incident with an "extreme case where the laws become inadequate even to their own preservation, and where the universal resource is a dictator, or martial law" (Jefferson quoted in Levy 1963, 18). This attitude stood in marked contrast to the position he formerly expressed in his *Notes on the State of Virginia* that dictatorship of any kind and at any time "was treason against the people; was treason against mankind in general; as rivetting for ever the chains which bow down their necks, by giving to their oppressors a proof, which they would have trumpeted through the universe, of the imbecility of republican government, in times of pressing danger, to shield them from harm" (91).

Jefferson's conclusions about Burr may or may not have been justified, but his willingness to manipulate the American system of justice was inexcusable. Relying heavily on the testimony of the two-faced Wilkinson, he became convinced of Burr's guilt and naturally was disappointed with the jury's verdict. Yet disappointment is one thing; abusing the law to vindicate one's views and satisfy one's ego is quite another. Former President John Adams noted that if Burr's "guilt is as clear as the noonday sun, the first magistrate of the nation ought not to have pronounced it so before a jury had tried him" (Adams quoted in Peterson 1970, 853). Future President Andrew Jackson said that the trial "assumed the shape of political persecution" (Jackson quoted in Levy 1963, 75). Leonard Levy observes that Jefferson's "object was not to secure justice by having Burr's guilt—or innocence—firmly determined, but to secure a conviction, no matter how, on the charge of high treason" (71). He concludes that Jefferson "was insensible to constitutional limitations and to standards of fairness" (70).

Merrill Peterson, one of Jefferson's most sympathetic biographers, offers the following measured view of the whole affair:

> The verdict of common sense, of morality, and of history on Burr was, and must remain, guilty; the verdict of law was, and must remain, innocent. He might have been convicted on a less stringent interpretation of the treason clause, and but for Marshall's political bias this would surely have been the result. In the long run, however, the nation was better served by his bias than by Jefferson's. For conviction would have introduced into American law the ancient English principle of "constructive treason," founded in this case on Burr's "constructive presence" at Blennerhassett's Island, where the evidence failed to pin overt acts of treason on him. It was better that the scoundrel go free than be convicted on evidence outside the indictment or on a constructive definition of the act of "levying war." (Peterson 1970, 873).

FRANKLIN D. ROOSEVELT
AND THE JAPANESE EXCLUSION ACT

Yet another prime example of this sort of cynical presidential behavior involved Franklin Delano Roosevelt and the Japanese Exclusion Act of 1942. In February 1942 FDR signed an order permitting the army to move over 100,000 Japanese Americans from the West Coast to inland locations where they remained under armed guard for the duration of World War II. Two-thirds of the evacuees were U.S. citizens. All this happened despite the fact that "there was not one demonstrable case of sabotage or espionage committed in the continental United States by a Japanese-American during the entire war" (Daniels 1975, 12). Many historians agree with Doris Kearns Goodwin that the Japanese exclusion represents "the worst single wholesale violation of civil rights of American citizens in our history" (Goodwin 1994, 321).

Even before Pearl Harbor the Japanese were not welcomed guests to our shores. Relations between the two countries did not begin until 1853 when Commodore Matthew Perry opened Japan up for American trade. At the turn of the twentieth century the first significant wave of Japanese immigrants came here in response to adverse economic conditions at home and the need for cheap manual labor on the West Coast (The Commission 1982, 30). The obvious cultural, religious, language, and physical differences that separated the newcomers from the native population, as well as their willingness to work for lower wages, led to anti-Japanese sentiment almost immediately.

In 1905 the Japanese Exclusion League was formed by organized labor groups in San Francisco. Due to the influence of the league's approximately 100,000 members, the San Francisco School Board sought to segregate classrooms so that, the board declared, "our children would not be placed in any position where their youthful impression may be affected by association with pupils of the Mongolian race" (33). In 1907 President Theodore Roosevelt decided that the best way to handle this ugliness and ensure that it did not get any worse was to negotiate a "Gentlemen's Agreement" with Japan to restrict direct immigration between the two countries.

In 1913 racist xenophobia again reared its ugly head with the passage of the Webb-Heney Act by the California State Legislature, which prevented land sales to Japanese aliens. When Japan began to assert itself militarily in the 1930s by invading China, leaving the League of Nations, violating the 1921 Five Power Treaty on Naval Disarmament, and bombing an American gunboat on the Yangtze River, fear of what had become known as "the yellow peril" was heightened. The Japanese people were portrayed in books, movies, and newspapers as "sneaky, treacherous agents of a militaristic Japan seeking to control the West Coast" (37).

This, then, was the heritage of racial hatred toward Japanese immigrants (Issei) and their native-born children (Nisei) that prevailed in the United States when Japan attacked Pearl Harbor at dawn on December 7, 1941. A number of Americans, who had once decried the racism as immoral and irrational, now had second thoughts. Their growing hostility was fueled by radio and neswspaper reports warning of imminent enemy attacks aided and abetted by Japanese living in the Pacific states. "We have thousands of Japanese here," the Los Angeles Times editorialized on December 8. "Some, perhaps, many are . . . good Americans. What the rest may be we do not know, nor can we take a chance in light of yesterday's demonstration that treachery and double- dealing are major Japanese weapons" (Daniels 1975, 12).

On December 15 the secretary of the navy, Frank Knox, claimed, evidence to the contrary notwithstanding, that spies among the Japanese citizens living in Hawaii made the attack on Pearl Harbor possible. Before long Knox's spurious claims were adopted by such mainland groups as the American Legion and the Los Angeles Chamber of Commerce, which urged Congress to pass laws calling for the forced evacuation and internment of all people of Japanese descent on the West Coast (Myer 1972, 17). Although the Department of Justice in Washington, with Attorney General Francis Biddle and FBI Chief J. Edgar Hoover taking the lead, opposed such action as being impractical and unnecessary for national security, the War Department started applying pressure for mass arrests. At the beginning of 1942 General John De Witt, commanding officer of the army's Western Defense Command, Provost Marshal Allen Guillon, the army's principal law enforcement officer, and Major Karl Bendetsen, Guillon's deputy, formally requested Secretary of War Henry Stimson and Assistant Secretary John McCloy to transfer control over the fate of Japanese Americans from civilian to military authorities.

Now the racist ball really started to roll. By the end of January Stimson had convinced Biddle to approve De Witt's plan for establishing certain zones in the United States from which enemy aliens were to be excluded. On February 13, U.S. Representative Clarence Lea sent a communiqué to FDR on behalf of the entire West Coast congressional delegation recommending "the immediate evacuation of all persons of Japanese lineage and all others, aliens and citizens alike, whose presence shall be deemed dangerous or inimical to the defense of the United States from all strategic areas." How did they define "strategic areas"? Lea included the states of California, Oregon, Washington, and Arizona, and the territory of Alaska on his list (The Commission 1982, 81).

On February 19, FDR finally relented. He signed Executive Order 9066 directing Stimson "to prescribe military areas in such places and of such extent as he or the appropriate military commander may determine, from which any or all persons may be excluded." The next day Stimson named De Witt to administer the exclusions (Myer 1972, 23). While Roosevelt and Stimson did not explicitly mention Japanese Americans, it was clear to everyone concerned that their directives applied exclusively to them and not to Germans and Italians, for example (The Commission 1982, 85).

On March 22 the forced removal began of every Japanese person from the three Pacific states and the southern part of Arizona. No one, not even the elderly or orphaned children, was spared. Homes that had been lived in for generations and businesses that took a lifetime to build were lost virtually overnight. By 1946, when the exclusion ended, 110,316 people whose only crime was their racial heritage had been sent to relocation centers and internment camps in such places as Manzanar and Tule Lake, California; Poston, Arizona; Topaz, Utah; Minidoka, Idaho; and Jerome, Arkansas (Myer 1972, 315).

What was FDR thinking? Why would a president who acted so prudently during much of World War II now make such a cynical decision? We will never know for sure, but some scholars speculate that he felt the need for full support of his New Deal reforms and the war effort and hence shied away from alienating Congress, the military, and influential segments of the American population. Since an incredible amount of pressure was being placed on him by members of these groups to exclude the Japanese, who lacked political power of their own at the time, it would have been easier to neglect them in favor of their opponents (Daniels 1975, 45). FDR used a similar rationalization to justify his reluctance to support the civil rights of African Americans and protect the lives of European Jews. Of course, there is nothing he could have said or done to excuse the serious miscarriage of justice that Executive Order 9066 represents. It simply is immoral to deny people their freedom and individuality by judging them according to racial stereotypes.

An interesting sidelight to the Japanese exclusion issue is how it demonstrates the fragility and fleeting nature of prudent leadership on the part of FDR and other influential Americans. As chief justice of the United States from 1953 to 1968, Earl Warren often was an exemplar of prudential jurisprudence. As California attorney general in 1942, he actively supported the relocation and internment. For over forty years Walter Lippmann was one of our most respected journalists. In 1942 Lippmann wrote a syndicated newspaper column entitled "The Fifth Column on the Coast" in which "he advocated setting aside the civil rights of citizens of Japanese ancestry" (Myer 1972, 22). In the 1962 *Engle v. Vitale* United States Supreme Court decision, Justice Tom Clark offered a prudent approach to the public school prayer controversy. Twenty years earlier he had been a Department of Justice official who was unable to support Attorney General Biddle's opposition to the exclusion. Justice Hugo Black is widely considered to be one of the greatest defenders of civil liberties in American history. In the 1944 *Korematsu v. United States* decision, however, he wrote:

> We uphold the exclusion order as of the time it was made and when the petitioner violated it. In so doing, we are not unmindful of the hardships imposed by it upon a large group of American citizens. But hardships are part of war, and war is an aggregation of hardships. All citizens alike, both in and out of uniform, feel the impact of war in greater or lesser measure. Citizenship has its responsibilities as well as its privileges, and in time of war the burden is always heavier. Compulsory exclusion of large groups of citizens from their homes, except under circumstances of direst emergency and peril, is inconsistent with our basic governmental institutions. But when under conditions of modern warfare our shores are threatened by hostile forces, the power to protect must be commensurate with the threatened danger. (323 U.S. 219–20)

BILL CLINTON'S SEXUAL MISCONDUCT

The essence of cynical behavior is its utter selfishness. Nixon subverted the American political process in order to win the 1972 presidential election. Jefferson's personal hatred for Aaron Burr led him to manipulate and exploit the very legal system he helped to create. FDR signed the Japanese Exclusion Act because he was unwilling to directly confront the challenge of powerful interests to his leadership during World War II. Bill Clinton jeopardized his own authority and the authority of future chief executives for the sake of instant sexual gratification.

During the 1992 presidential campaign a Little Rock, Arkansas, woman by the name of Gennifer Flowers told the tabloids that she had had a twelve-year-long affair with Clinton. Hillary Clinton subsequently joined her husband on television's *60 Minutes* to deny Flowers's story. In 1994 an Arkansas state employee, Paula Jones, accused Clinton of making unwanted sexual advances toward her while he was governor. When Clinton claimed the incident never occurred, she sued him for sexual harassment and emotional distress. Clinton's subsequent argument that sitting presidents cannot be defendants in civil lawsuits was rejected by the United States Supreme Court.

Then in 1997 Linda Tripp, a former White House aide, released tapes of conversations she secretly recorded with Monica Lewinsky in which Lewinsky confessed to having sex with Clinton while serving as an unpaid presidential intern. When Jones's lawyers sought to use her confessions as evidence in their case, Lewinsky promptly disavowed them. In the course of being deposed for the Jones suit, furthermore, Clinton declared the original Lewinsky allegations to be untrue, but admitted to having had sex with Flowers.

Meanwhile, back in 1994 Attorney General Janet Reno had appointed Kenneth Starr, a former solicitor general in the Bush administration, to the post of independent counsel to investigate a possible Clinton connection to the Whitewater, Arkansas, financial scandal involving a failed land deal and the related collapse of a savings and loan bank that cost federal taxpayers $60 million. Now Starr sought to subpoena both Lewinsky and the president himself to discover whether there had been pressure from the White House, in the form of threats, job promises, and hush money, to get Lewinsky to recant her story. With her help, he hoped to establish a pattern of behavior to confirm his suspicion that Clinton similarly had abused the power of the presidency to lie under oath, suborn perjury, intimidate witnesses, and obstruct justice in the Whitewater probe and at various other times while he was in office. There also was talk of possible impeachment hearings if Starr could prove his allegations in a report he expected to deliver to Congress in September 1998.

When, in the spring of 1998, the congressional deadline for the Whitewater investigation was reached, Reno appointed a three-judge panel that in turn authorized Starr to continue his four-year $50 million inquiry (Pooley 1998, 148). At this point the tide really began to turn against

Clinton. In short order, federal courts ruled against his claims that law-yer-client and executive privileges prohibited Starr from questioning presi-dential counsels and Secret Service agents about their knowledge of the Lewinsky affair; under oath and protection of full immunity from prosecu-tion Lewinsky admitted to a sexual relationship with Clinton in the Oval Office but declined to implicate him in the subornation of perjury; and the American people witnessed the spectacle of a sitting president essentially substantiating her testimony before a grand jury via closed-circuit televi-sion from the White House. Moreover, during a special prime-time public broadcast on the evening of August 17, 1998, using legal doubletalk that tended to obfuscate the issue, Clinton acknowledged that he had misled his family, friends, and the nation about the nature of his association with Lewinsky and attacked Starr for what he claimed was an overzealous, po-litically biased investigation into his private life.

Calls for impeachment proceedings or congressional censure heated up with the publication of the Starr Report on September 11 and the release of Clinton's rebuttal shortly thereafter. In response to the often salacious evi-dence presented by Starr against him, Clinton argued that while the affair with Lewinsky was a personal failing on his part, it did not fit the constitu-tional definition of an impeachable offense. As his lawyer, David Kendall, put it: "No amount of gratuitous allegations about his relationship with Ms. Lewinsky, no matter how graphic, can alter the fact that the president did not commit perjury, he did not obstruct justice, he did not tamper with witnesses, and he did not abuse the power of his office" (Solomon 1998, 4A).

On December 19, 1998, the events of six long years finally came to a head. For only the second time in American history the House of Representatives impeached a president. The charges brought against Clinton were that he lied under oath to Starr's grand jury about his relationship with Lewinsky and obstructed justice by encouraging his friends and aides to cover up the affair. In the subsequent trial, over which the Supreme Court Chief Justice, William Rehnquist, presided, the Senate voted to acquit on almost strictly partisan lines. Although the senators generally expressed their disdain for what they considered to be his morally reprehensible activities, the re-quired two-thirds majority could not agree that his activities constituted, as Alexander Hamilton wrote in *Federalist #65*, "political . . . injuries done im-mediately to the society itself" (Madison, Hamilton, and Jay 1961, 396).

The irony is that as more and more allegations about Clinton's sexual misconduct were revealed, his popularity ratings climbed. A March 30, 1998, *Time* magazine poll found that 67 percent of Americans felt Clinton was doing a good job, a figure that lowered only to 61 percent after his Au-gust 17 broadcast (Gibbs and Duffy 1998, 31) and to 62 percent after the release of the Starr Report (Lester 1998, 4A). Since 52 percent also thought he "lacks the proper moral character to be President" (Gibbs 1998, 21), some commentators concluded that as long as the economy ran smoothly Americans would continue to agree with Clinton that his behavior was politically irrelevant.

Yet the evidence suggests that Clinton had indeed allowed his alleged sexual indiscretions to interfere with his performance as president. As Haynes Johnson and David Broder indicate, as far back as 1994 it was the unwillingness of the American people to trust him that contributed to the defeat of his health care initiative (Johnson and Broder 1996, 543). The argument can also be made that Clinton's crisis of confidence influenced the way he conducted foreign policy and interfered with his plans to reform such significant social programs as Social Security and public education. According to Erwin Hargrove's interpretation of Aristotelian prudence, a leader "is more likely to succeed at persuasion when he has personal credibility with his audience, making him more believable than others. This is especially the case when certainty is impossible and opinions are divided. Character is the best means of persuasion that a good man possesses" (Hargrove 1998, 186).

Perhaps the most disturbing legacy of Clinton's behavior is the way it may have soured us on the office and unreasonably lowered our expectations of presidential leadership. In 1874 Grover Cleveland was identified as the father of an illegitimate son. Cleveland denied the charges and refused to marry the mother, but agreed to support them financially. When the Democratic party was considering whether to nominate him to run for president against the Republican James Blaine in 1884, one observer remarked:

> We are told that Mr. Blaine has been delinquent in office but blameless in private life, while Mr. Cleveland has been a model of official integrity, but culpable in his personal relations. We should therefore elect Mr. Cleveland to the public office which he is so well qualified to fill, and remand Mr. Blaine to the private station which he is admirably fitted to adorn. (Nevins 1932, 1: 167)

Was Cleveland, an honest adulterer who wound up doing a credible job as president, the only real option Americans had to Blaine, who as Speaker of the House of Representatives took kickbacks from railroad companies?

Warren G. Harding had at least two extramarital affairs. One woman, Nan Britton, conceived his daughter and continued having sex with him while he was president—sometimes in a closet converted for just that purpose in the White House (Russell 1968, 466). Like Clinton, the Harding ad-

ministration was marked by a strong economy. Have we finally accepted
the normalization of Harding's ethics? The trust of children in the American political system was severely shaken by Watergate. What are the children thinking now? Have successful leaders with high moral character
become mere figments of our imagination? Proponents of Aristotelian prudence refuse to allow their standards to fall so low. Since they believe that
human beings have the potential to be moral or immoral and rational or irrational, they are neither shocked by the Cleveland and Harding scandals
nor surprised by Lincoln's statesmanship during the Civil War.

In an analysis of prudent political leadership, a discussion of sexual misconduct by presidents is appropriate because for Aristotle a critical connection exists between prudence and moral behavior. "The man who is
passion's slave," Aristotle argues, is unable to fully appreciate and honestly follow moral ideals, much less develop the talent to reconcile them
with material circumstances (Aristotle 1966, 310). "Vice gives a twist to our
minds, making us hold false opinions about the principles of ethics," he
writes. "It is therefore obvious that a man cannot be prudent unless he be
good" (190). We are reminded that, while Aristotle is unwilling to make
prudence synonymous with personal virtue, he does maintain that it
serves along with political acumen as necessary preconditions for prudent
leadership.

Yet the specter of presidents repeatedly cheating on their spouses represents the antithesis of virtuous behavior. Only a person acting like a cynic
would continue to seek cheap thrills at the expense of his family, his presidency, and his nation. Clinton, who had been maintaining all along that a
president's personal life is nobody's business but his own, nevertheless
acknowledged the legitimacy of Aristotle's position during a speech to an
audience of students at Beijing University on June 28, 1998. "The struggle
for your own character," Clinton said, " is the struggle for the nation's character" (Gough 1998, 13A).

As political scientist Walter Dean Burnham observes, the fact that separation of church and state prevails in the United States places additional
pressure on presidents. Since we lack a pope, archbishop of Canterbury, or
chief rabbi, Burnham argues, the role of "high priest of American civil religion" necessarily falls on their shoulders and requires them to serve as our
official moral exemplars (Burnham 1997, 17). What further complicates the
situation is the existence of competing twenty-four-hour news networks
that severely minimizes the amount of privacy presidents can expect to enjoy. Like it or not, these are among the conditions of contemporary presidential life. That Clinton was well aware of these conditions when he

assumed office only serves to underscore the level of his recklessness and the quality of his imprudence.

Americans who supported Clinton in 1992 and 1996 were led to believe that he was dedicated to serving the public interest of the United States at a crucial time in our history. By acting again and again like an undisciplined man who likes to take unfair advantage of women and enjoys trying to get away with outrageous behavior, however, he compromised his effectiveness as a leader and set dangerous precedents for future presidents. Due to Clinton's pattern of philandering, presidents can now be sued while in office for private conduct; a president's claim to obtain confidential advice from aides and government lawyers has been damaged; and presidents may be hesitant about letting Secret Service agents get close enough to do their job for fear that the agents will be compelled to testify against them.

Andrew Jackson's role in the forced removal of the Cherokee people from Georgia, the brutal and callous 1836 "Trail of Tears," and Lyndon Johnson's 1964 Tonkin Gulf resolution, which deliberately deceived Congress and the American people about the nature of U.S. involvement in Southeast Asia, constitute other examples of presidential cynicism. In each of these cases self-vindicating and self-indulgent decisions on the part of chief executives diminished their leadership skills and led to the abandonment of some of our most cherished ideals.

By definition, presidents acting idealistically or with prudence would not have participated in such blatantly immoral activities. It is logically possible to imagine pragmatists committing these errors of judgment during moments of weakness. In order to be consistently pragmatic, however, they would have had to take actions that Nixon, Jefferson, FDR, Clinton, Jackson, and Lyndon Johnson neglected to take. Once the American people began to recognize their behavior as imprudent, pragmatic leaders would have immediately attempted to salvage their presidencies by changing their attitudes and policies, sincerely admitting their mistakes, and asking the voters for forgiveness. During the Lewinsky affair, unfortunately, Bill Clinton chose the cynical alternative. He spent more time attacking Kenneth Starr than owning up to his own personal failings.

CHAPTER 6

Pragmatic Presidential Leadership

HARRY TRUMAN AND THE ATOMIC BOMB

Cynicism involves the complete abandonment of ideals. When presidents act pragmatically, on the other hand, they do not abandon ideals so much as deemphasize them. According to William James, one of the intellectual founders of pragmatism in the United States, even ideals have a "cash value" that can be determined by "its payoff in action" (Ryan 1999, 10). As James writes: "Now pragmatism, devoted though she be to facts, has no such materialistic bias as ordinary empiricism labors under. Moreover, she has no objection whatever to the realizing of abstractions, so long as you get about among particulars with their aid and they actually carry you somewhere" (James 1950, 20–21). It was just this sort of thinking, stressing tangible results but not to the exclusion of intangible values, that convinced Harry Truman to drop the atomic bomb on Japan at the end of World War II.

After FDR's sudden death in April 1945, the immediate problem facing his successor, Harry Truman, was how to bring World War II to a close. When Germany gave up one month later, attention was focused on the hostilities in the Pacific. Although Japan had virtually no navy or air force left at the time, it was not yet clear if and when it would finally admit defeat. The kamikaze fight to the death mentality displayed by Japanese soldiers in places such as Iwo Jima and Okinawa led some military analysts to predict that it would cost an additional million American lives to invade the mainland of Japan (Wyden 1984, 132). In 1939 emigre scientists such as Albert Einstein convinced FDR to establish the top secret Manhattan Project to beat the Nazis to the punch in developing an unprecedented weapon of mass destruction called the atomic bomb. With its successful testing at Alamogordo, New Mexico, in July 1945, the weapon became available for Truman's use.

Japan's fierce national pride and anxiety about the fate of Emperor Hirohito made it reluctant to voluntarily accept the terms of unconditional surrender. Truman could have cynically ignored these factors and, without warning, concern for Japanese civilian losses, or even a trace of remorse, bombed them into oblivion. At Yalta in February 1945 FDR had brokered a deal with Stalin that the Soviet Union would wage war on Japan once Germany was defeated in return for land concessions in the Far East. From a cynical perspective the advantages of remorselessly dropping the atomic bomb on Japan were to bring the war to an abrupt end, save American lives, claim vengeance for Pearl Harbor, and justify our reneging on the land concessions to Stalin because his military support was no longer necessary. Furthermore, through the cynical decimation of entire cities Truman could have planned to frighten the Soviet Union into moderating its postwar foreign policy objectives.

Nuclear weapons are more than just extraordinarily powerful military devices. Their ability to unleash the elementary forces of nature for such destructive purposes makes them qualitatively different from other mechanisms of war. Knowing this, Truman could have idealistically refused to give in to revenge, prohibited use of the bomb at any time for any reason, insisted on a negotiated settlement that allowed Japan to retain its royal family, and honored FDR's deal with Stalin. Idealism, moreover, would have required the United States to share the secrets of the atom with its allies, including the Soviet Union. Fully expecting that Stalin could be trusted and that permanent world peace was at hand, Truman could have established an international partnership as early as 1945 based on the dream of developing atomic energy for peaceful ends and limiting the proliferation of nuclear weapons.

On the other hand, Truman could have made the prudential decision to explode a demonstration bomb in the Sea of Japan or some other unpopulated area to shift the burden of moral proof over to the Japanese by letting them know what was in store for them if they did not soon surrender. He then could have sweetened the pot and permitted them to save face by promising not to prosecute their emperor. If Japan still refused to relent, Truman could have given the order in relatively good conscience to use the bomb to incinerate military installations located on the Japanese mainland. There would have been civilian casualties to be sure, but at this point Truman could say honestly and honorably that enough was enough. Too many American soldiers already had been lost in fighting a war they did not initiate and for which the United States was not directly responsible.

What would have been the prudent way to treat Stalin and the Soviet Union? Although in 1945 Truman was unaware that Soviet spies had infiltrated the Manhattan Project, he should have realized that the United States was not going to be able to protect its nuclear secrets forever. In an attempt to forestall a future doomsday arms race, therefore, Truman should have authorized the land concessions to the Soviet Union and made the principles of nuclear technology available to the world scientific community. Aristotelian prudence demands that political leaders resist illusions even as they strive to make the most ethical decisions possible under often trying circumstances. Stalin clearly was a mass murderer and treacherous foe of free government everywhere. Nevertheless, Truman was required by the standards of prudence to do his best to foster as much international cooperation as the world situation in 1945 would bear. He should have realized, in other words, that control over nuclear weapons can sometimes be derived from joint action as well as from conflict.

At the time some presidential advisors expressed the fear that alerting the Japanese to a demonstration bombing would doom the mission to failure and result in additional American casualties. Others feared that the new technology would misfire and make the United States look foolish. These fears were erroneous, however. By 1945 Japanese air defenses were essentially nonexistent. And the idea that we would prefer to test such a weapon over populated areas rather than over water does not speak too highly of American character.

In the spring and summer of 1945 there actually were a number of Americans who defended the prudential alternative. Among them were Army Chief of Staff General George Marshall and Under Secretary of the Navy Ralph Bard. Although Marshall admitted to being confused about exactly how to use the bomb, at a May 31 meeting of the "Interim Committee," appointed by Truman to advise him on these matters, he argued that Soviet scientists should be allowed to witness the Alamogordo test (Wyden 1984, 159). Bard was the only member of the committee to go on record opposing the no advance warning policy. Before resigning from his position in protest on July 1, he issued the following memorandum:

Ever since I have been in touch with this program, I have had the feeling that before the bomb is actually used against Japan that Japan should have some preliminary warning for say two or three days in advance of use. The position of the United States as a great humanitarian nation and the fair play attitude of our people generally is responsible in the main for this feeling.

During recent weeks I have also had the feeling very definitely that the Japanese government may be searching for some opportunity which they could use as a medium for surrender. Following the three-power conference (at Potsdam) emissaries from this country could contact representatives from Japan somewhere on the China coast and make representations with regard to Russia's position and at the same time give them information regarding the proposed use of atomic power, together with whatever assurances the President might care to make with regard to the Emperor of Japan and the treatment of the Japanese nation following unconditional surrender. It seems quite possible to me that this presents the opportunity which the Japanese are looking for. (Bard quoted in Alperovitz 1995, 225–26)

Marshall and Bard represented the minority view, however. On the advice of such people as Secretary of State James Byrnes and the chief of the Manhattan Project, Brigadier General Leslie Groves, Truman decided to take the pragmatic route. Thus, with some regret but without either warning Japan or adequately confiding in Stalin, a nuclear device was detonated at 8:15 A.M. on August 6 over the city of Hiroshima, a militarily insignificant target in the central Japanese island of Honshu at the western end of the Inland Sea. Close to 80,000 residents perished immediately or were so badly injured that they died within hours. The device had the power of 20,000 tons of TNT and, according to American fliers who participated in the bombing mission, produced a glare brighter than the sun (Malone and Rauch 1965, 79). When the Japanese failed to respond, a second blast occurred three days later over Nagasaki in the southern Japanese island of Kyushu, killing an additional 36,000 (Knebel and Bailey 1960, 181). In the aftermath Stalin declared war on Japan and invaded Manchuria. By August 10 Japan's leaders finally agreed to accept unconditional terms of surrender.

The lack of emphasis that Truman placed on moral ideals with regard to the bomb was a reflection of American frustration about the course of the war. We desperately wanted our children, spouses, siblings, and friends to come home and our lives to return to normal. Billions of dollars and years of effort had gone into the construction of a weapon that could stop the fighting and it did not seem unreasonable at the time to use it (McCullough 1992, 378). Everyone knew in 1945 that it was only a matter of time before the Japanese surrendered. When they delayed the inevitable, it did not seem unreasonable to punish them for their intransigence. Since Stalin was breaking the deals he made with FDR at Yalta concerning the independence of countries in Eastern Europe, it did not seem unreasonable to try to scare him into compliance, distrust his motives in the Far East, and refuse to share with him our nuclear secrets.

Yet Truman's pragmatism, which seemed to make sense at the time, proved to be unrealistic in the long run. Although Truman refused to seriously negotiate the status of Emperor Hirohito before the bomb was dropped, he wound up allowing Hirohito to stay in office afterward. Although Truman was highly suspicious of Stalin's motives before the bomb was dropped, he allowed Stalin to exert considerable power both in Eastern Europe and the Far East afterward. When Stalin eventually developed his own nuclear weapon, moreover, the United States and the Soviet Union entered into a cold war that over a forty-year period repeatedly brought the world to the brink of nuclear catastrophe.

There is no getting around the fact that the United States inaugurated the atomic age and remains the only country to employ its ultimate weapon. Perhaps the most negative effect on Americans of Truman's pragmatic inattention to moral considerations was that it seemed to bring us down to the level of our adversaries. As Leo Szilard, one of the scientists who joined with Einstein in persuading FDR to launch the Manhattan Project, observed:

> Suppose Germany had developed two bombs before we had any bombs. And suppose Germany had dropped one bomb, say, on Rochester and the other on Buffalo, and then having run out of bombs she would have lost the war. Can anyone doubt that we would then have defined the dropping of atomic bombs on cities as a war crime, and that we would have sentenced the Germans who were guilty of this crime to death at Nuremberg and hanged them? (Szilard 1960, 70)

Before the bomb was dropped, in short, Americans firmly believed we were fighting a righteous war as a nation at least striving to be righteous. Afterward, we could no longer be so sure. "If I had only known" what would transpire, Einstein lamented, "I would have been a locksmith." On August 7 the *St. Louis Post-Dispatch* editorialized that we had "signed the mammalian world's death warrant and deeded an earth in ruins to the ants," and the *Washington Post* likened Hiroshima to "the worst imaginary horrors of science fiction" (McCullough 1992, 456). By using the bomb, journalist Hanson Baldwin concluded, we became "inheritors of the mantle of Genghis Khan and all those of past history who have justified the use of utter ruthlessness in war" (Baldwin 1950, 102).

DWIGHT EISENHOWER AND MCCARTHYISM

Among cynical political leaders, the most dangerous is the demagogue. Demagogues are like rats and cockroaches that come out of the woodwork when we are in disarray and our homes are a mess. Demagogues appear when citizens begin to lose confidence in the power of their government to deal effectively with crucial social, economic, and political problems. By offering simplistic solutions to these problems, they hope to manipulate anxious citizens into granting them absolute power. Characteristically, the demagogues' solutions involve scapegoats and a jingoistic foreign policy. Among the most infamous demagogues in world history were Hitler, Mussolini, and Evita Peron.

According to Aristotle, demagogues are most likely to appear in what he calls "extreme democracies" (Aristotle 1962, 234). The citizens of these societies take the democratic ideal of equality literally. In other words, they consider all people to be equal in all respects and all norms to be equally valid. When no societal norm is preferred to any other, however, citizens begin to experience feelings of aimlessness and a condition known as anomie sets in. Since citizens have an extremely difficult time living well in an anomic environment that refuses to provide them with guidance from established societal norms, they engage in a frenetic search for help from whomever is willing to supply it.

Enter the demagogues, whom Aristotle refers to as "the courtiers of democracy" (245). Their appeal is that they are more than willing to fill the moral vacuum created by "extreme democracies." To the extent that they are successful, demagogues possess an extraordinary spiritual power to evoke support. The problem is that their charisma blinds citizens to the demagogues' plans to replace the rule of law with lawlessness and democracy with tyranny. As Aristotle writes, "the record of history attests the fact . . . that most tyrants have begun their careers as demagogues" (235).

There have been numerous demagogues in American history, including Huey Long, George Wallace, and Louis Farrakhan, but the most dangerous by far was Joseph McCarthy. McCarthy served as a Republican senator from Wisconsin from 1946 until his death in 1957. During most of that time he utilized the age-old tactics of demagoguery to influence the formation and execution of American domestic and foreign policies. His manipulative powers derived from the nature of the cold war. Here were two superpowers, possessing the nuclear capability to destroy the earth in an instant, involved in a clash of diametrically opposed ideologies. The American people were genuinely frightened by the situation and McCarthy was able to exploit their fear by participating in the creation of a national anti-Communist hysteria that served his purposes.

On February 9, 1950, McCarthy told a Woman's Republican Club in Wheeling, West Virginia, that he could name 205 people in the State Department who were permitted to retain their jobs even though Secretary of State Dean Acheson knew they were Communists. The next day in Salt Lake City, Utah, he made essentially the same speech except that the number of known Communists was reduced to 57. When challenged either to name specific names or retract his accusations, McCarthy identified Owen Lattimore, a professor of Far Eastern Studies at the Johns Hopkins University who had served as an advisor to the State Department, as "the top Russian espionage agent" in the United States (McCarthy quoted in Rovere 1967, 151).

As McCarthy demonstrated in the Lattimore case, his lists of Communists were composed exclusively of Americans who disagreed with his jingoistic politics and witch hunt methods. There clearly were dangerous subversives at large in this country during the 1950s. But Joseph McCarthy would have been the last person to discover them because he was more interested in serving his own interests than the public interest of the United States. In the investigations of Lattimore that followed, both the FBI and a Senate subcommittee chaired by Millard Tydings of Maryland found McCarthy's allegations to be essentially groundless. McCarthy reacted typically by accusing Tydings of being a Communist sympathizer, an accusation he realized would serve to defeat Tydings in the 1950 senatorial elections.

In 1951 McCarthy charged that General George Marshall was part of a Communist "conspiracy so immense and an infamy so black as to dwarf any previous venture in the history of man" (McCarthy quoted in Oshinsky 1985, 197). Now Marshall already has been referred to in this book as a person who could appreciate the value of prudent leadership. For instance, he recognized as early as 1945 the need for the United States to cooperate with the Soviet Union on the subject of nuclear weapons. He was one of the authors of the fabled Marshall Plan, which strengthened Western Europe economically so it could successfully resist attempted Communist takeovers after World War II. He served with distinction as chief of staff of the American Armed Services under FDR and as secretaries of state and defense under Truman. He won the Nobel Peace Prize in 1953. He was approached by both Democrats and Republicans to run for president, but declined, owing to his belief in the strict separation between politics and the military. Of Marshall, indeed, it has been said, "No other American in our history can be imagined who could have taken over command from General Washington at Valley Forge" (Acheson 1969, 213).

The intellectual basis for Marshall's insights and achievements was his comprehension of what Aristotle considers to be the prudent connection between power and morality. "Throughout his career he was forced to deal with different aspects, complexities, ironies, nuances, and contradictions of power as the United States continued to amass it," historian Mark Stoler writes:

> While the theologian Reinhold Niebuhr was attempting to explain these to an American people unprepared for global responsibilities, Marshall, by his actions and beliefs, became the incarnation of the leader who learned to understand them and to act accordingly. Power was not limitless or divisible, appearances to the contrary notwithstanding. Its military, political, and economic aspects could not be divorced from each other. Nor could they be equated, or renounced in an effort to maintain a state of moral purity. In the imperfect world of human beings, each had to be accepted, understood, coordinated, and made to serve the goals of a rational and ethical policy. That required the creation and implementation of specific strategies that appropriately linked available means with desired ends and that reinforced rather than challenged the most cherished values of American society. (Stoler 1989, ix–x)

For years the relationship between Marshall and Dwight Eisenhower had been extremely close. After acting as Eisenhower's personal and professional mentor for many years, it was Marshall who recommended his promotion to supreme commander of the Allied Forces in Europe, a position that Marshall initially had wanted for himself. During Eisenhower's command, moreover, it had been Marshall who ordered him to end his affair with his driver, Kay Summersby. In the book *Plain Speaking*, biographer Merle Miller quotes Harry Truman as saying that Marshall warned his friend of the tragic consequences that would befall both him and the nation if he neglected to avoid even the appearance of sexual impropriety. Appearance counts, Marshall argued. With the very existence of the free world depending on his leadership, Eisenhower could not risk diverting public attention from the crucial task at hand (Miller 1974, 340).

When Eisenhower announced his candidacy for president in 1952 and subsequently won the election hands down, therefore, some Americans were confident that he would use his newfound "bully pulpit" to publicly denounce McCarthy and defend the honor of a person he earlier had extolled as "the strongest weapon that I have always had in my hand" (Stoler

1989, 129). On the campaign trail in McCarthy's home state of Wisconsin, however, Eisenhower demonstrated that this confidence was misplaced. In Milwaukee, with McCarthy on the podium behind him, he delivered an address that omitted any reference to Marshall. When the press, which had been given advance access to the full text of the speech, compared what Eisenhower said to the original wording, they reported that he had placated McCarthy by deleting the following passage:

> Let me be specific. I know that charges of disloyalty have, in the past, been leveled against General George C. Marshall. I have been privileged for thirty-five years to know General Marshall personally. I know him, as a man and as a soldier, to be dedicated with singular selflessness and the profoundest patriotism to the service of America. (Oshinsky 1985, 236)

Although there is no evidence to suggest that Marshall ever held a grudge for this deletion, the episode is significant because it illustrates what can happen when leaders fail to act responsibly. Marshall's stature was such that he really did not need Eisenhower's help. But thousands of other Americans, who were not as renowned as Marshall and whose only crime was that they did not agree with McCarthy, lost their jobs and had their reputations destroyed in part because influential Americans refused to stand up for them. As journalist Robert Shogan observes, "the net result" of Eisenhower's appeasement of McCarthy in the infamous Milwaukee incident was to boost "the stature of McCarthy by demonstrating that even Eisenhower was unwilling to challenge him" (Shogan 1999, 101).

Eisenhower continued to placate McCarthy after he took office. Angered in part by the army's refusal to give preferential treatment to a draftee who happened to be one of his aides, McCarthy in 1954 began attacking the institution for harboring Communist spies. During this incident, in which McCarthy called the commanding officer of Camp Kilmer, New Jersey, one of the heroes of D-day and the Battle of the Bulge, "a disgrace to the uniform . . . not fit to be an officer . . . (and) ignorant," Eisenhower again chose to remain in the background and not share his thoughts with the public (Rovere 167, 30). At the nationally televised Army-McCarthy hearings that ensued, the American people as a whole witnessed McCarthy's cynicism in the raw for the first time and turned against him. From then on McCarthy was dead politically. The Senate censured him for misbehavior on December 2, 1954, by a vote of 67 to 22. Long a heavy drinker, he died on May 2, 1957, of complications caused by cirrhosis of the liver.

Some students of the presidency, including Fred Greenstein, argue that what appeared to be a policy of passive appeasement by Eisenhower toward McCarthy actually was a carefully constructed strategy that served as an effective antidote to the demagogue's confrontational tactics. "I will not—I refuse—to get into the gutter" with him, Greenstein quotes Eisenhower as writing in his personal diary. "Senator McCarthy is, of course, so anxious for headlines that he is prepared to go to any extreme in order to secure some mention of his name in the public press. His actions create trouble on the Hill with members of his party; they irritate, frustrate, and infuriate members of the Executive Department. . . . I really believe that nothing will be so effective in combating this particular kind of trouble-making as to ignore him. This he cannot stand" (Greenstein 1982, 169). Greenstein observes that Eisenhower's decision to avoid direct opposition in favor of behind-the-scenes maneuvers, which included using patronage as a weapon, ultimately had the desired effect of bringing about McCarthy's demise. "It is difficult to see," Greenstein concludes, "how, at least for the purposes of defusing McCarthy, another technique would have worked faster and more decisively in the context of the time" (227).

Not surprisingly Emmet John Hughes, the speechwriter whose text Eisenhower edited in Wisconsin, reaches a different conclusion. One of the president's key roles, Hughes maintains, is to take an unmistakable stand on issues directly relating to democratic values—even if such a stand results in the temporary loss of popular support. A great democratic leader, Hughes writes, "must be pragmatic, calculating, and earthbound—and yet know when to spurn the mean arithmetic of expediency for the sake of utter courage, the sublime gamble that holds no hope beyond the audacity of his own imagination" (Hughes 1963, 98–99). In Hughes's estimation, Eisenhower's refusal to openly oppose McCarthy's bullying tactics and violation of the civil liberties of innocent Americans demonstrates that he lacked the moral courage necessary to be a great leader.

A similar point is made by Stephen Ambrose, who describes Eisenhower's indirect and covert approach as a pragmatic attempt to combine his disapproval of McCarthy's undemocratic methods with his need for right-wing votes in Congress. This example of Eisenhower's pragmatism, Ambrose argues, was "illustrative of (his) willingness to abandon principles when faced with practical problems of political resistance" (Ambrose 1984, 77). According to Ambrose:

Eisenhower wanted to see Senator McCarthy eliminated from national public life, and he wanted it done without making America's record and image on civil-liberties issues worse than it already was. But because Eisenhower would not denounce McCarthy by name, or otherwise stand up to the senator from Wisconsin, McCarthy was able to do much damage to civil liberties, the Republican Party, numerous individuals, the U.S. Army, and the Executive Branch before he finally destroyed himself. . . . Eisenhower's cautious, hesitant approach—or nonapproach—to the McCarthy issue did the President's reputation no good, and much harm. (1984, 620)

Ambrose also criticizes Eisenhower for claiming the absolute right to withhold from McCarthy information and advice given to him by his staff. "It is essential to efficient and effective administration that employees of the Executive Branch be in a position to be completely candid in advising with each other on official matters," Eisenhower wrote in 1954. Therefore "it is not in the public interest that any of their conversations or communications, or any documents or reproductions, concerning such advice be disclosed" (1984, 187–88). Although previous presidents, including George Washington, had invoked this power of executive privilege, none had applied it to all information in his possession and to all members of the executive branch. By proposing such an imprudent precedent, Ambrose charges, Eisenhower thought he had discovered a convenient way to simultaneously maintain the integrity of his office and escape the heat that a public condemnation of McCarthy's demagoguery would have generated. He also laid the legal groundwork for Richard Nixon's and Bill Clinton's later attempts to shield their improprieties from the prying eyes of special prosecutors.

Marshall had been Eisenhower's trusted mentor and friend. Prudent and idealistic presidents would never betray the trust of mentors and friends the same way Eisenhower did in Milwaukee. Idealists, moreover, would have attacked McCarthy on all fronts in a direct and straightforward manner regardless of the consequences. Prudent leaders would have strongly defended Marshall and resorted to more subtle, yet unmistakably public and undeniably firm, methods to assail McCarthy in other areas. For example, a president behaving prudently would have provided explicit support for McCarthy's critics during the Senate's Army-McCarthy hearings. Cynics, of course, have no trusted mentors and friends, only acquaintances they can manipulate and exploit. And cynics would never attack a person as powerful as McCarthy was in the early 1950s, either directly or indirectly, for fear of the effects such an attack might have on their own political aspirations.

JOHN F. KENNEDY AND THE BAY OF PIGS

When John F. Kennedy was inaugurated in 1961 he inherited plans laid during the Eisenhower administration for the invasion of Cuba. This turn of events was previously discussed in chapter 4. The issue in question here is the type of leadership Kennedy applied to the invasion plans once he found out about them. In the end Kennedy opted for pragmatic leadership, a decision that almost led to the outbreak of World War III.

Shortly after assuming power in 1959 Fidel Castro initiated a vitriolic campaign to demonize the United States. Given our inexcusable past treatment of his country, Castro found that anti-Americanism could serve as a convenient stimulus for the development of Cuban nationalism as well as the consolidation of his power. When Castro compounded the vitriol by threatening to sever U.S.-Cuban relations, declaring an adherence to Communist ideology, and establishing close ties to the Soviet Union, Eisenhower had enough. He concluded that coexistence with Castro was not feasible and resolved to launch a clandestine CIA operation against Cuba patterned after a similar 1954 undertaking in Guatemala (Smith 1987, 63).

For less than a year, starting in the summer of 1960, the CIA recruited and trained approximately 1,400 Cuban refugees for the attempted coup. The group of 1,400, calling itself Brigade 2506 after the serial number of a popular comrade killed during training in the Guatemalan jungles (Johnson 1964, 56), included members of the previous Batista government and a small number of professional soldiers (Barber 1992, 365). Their strategy was to have an invasion fleet escorted by U.S. Navy ships depart from Nicaragua and land on the southern coast of Cuba at the Bay of Pigs (Bahia de Cochinas). In order to ensure a safe landing, sixteen World War II B-26 Marauders flown by refugee pilots would precede the flotilla and wipe out what was supposed to be a small and ineffectual Cuban air force. Having once established a beachhead, the invaders were to link up with the domestic anti-Castro underground and, gaining followers along the way among civilians anxious to overthrow the Communist dictatorship, march north to victory in Havana. Should Castro's forces somehow prove capable of repelling Brigade 2506, it was expected that the American military would come to its rescue.

Upon taking office Kennedy had to decide what to do. He could have cynically proceeded with the invasion exactly as it had been concocted by the CIA and, without any pangs of conscience, contravened the charters of both the United Nations and the Organization of American States, which prohibit foreign military interference with the internal affairs of sovereign countries. He could have idealistically scrapped the invasion entirely and sought to persuade Castro to initiate democratic reforms in Cuba. He could have prudently scrapped the invasion and engaged Castro in a dialogue about the prospects for peaceful relations while working to support democratic factions within the domestic Cuban underground. Or he could have pragmatically split the difference between the CIA's plans for a full-fledged invasion and the moral and legal objections to it.

Kennedy chose the latter alternative. On April 4, 1961, he gave the official go-ahead with the proviso that no American forces participate in the operation once it reached Cuban soil. That meant no air and sea cover and no marines storming the beaches to come to the aid of besieged invaders. As Kennedy coyly announced in an April 12 press conference five days before the invasion took place:

> There will not be, under any conditions, an intervention in Cuba by the United States Armed Forces. . . . The basic issue in Cuba is not one between the United States and Cuba. It is between the Cubans themselves. I intend to see that we adhere to that principle and as I understand it this administration's attitude is so understood and shared by the anti-Castro exiles from Cuba in this country. (Kennedy quoted in Schlesinger 1967, 245)

Kennedy also hedged on the number of antiquated B-26s sent to eradicate the Cuban air force, cutting the total down from sixteen to eight (Szulc 1986, 604).

Things predictably began to fall apart from the moment the invaders landed in the early morning hours of April 17. The CIA had grossly underestimated the power of the Cuban military. The 1,400 members of Brigade 2506 were no match for the well-equipped and ably led 225,000-man Cuban army (602). Nor were the eight B-26s able to guarantee the safety of either the troops or their off-shore supply vessels from what turned out to be a surprisingly strong Cuban air force. On the other hand, the CIA had grossly overestimated the roles that the domestic anti-Castro underground and Cuban civilians would play in the attempted coup. Castro, who learned of the invasion in advance from spies in the Miami Cuban-American community, neutralized the underground by arresting and jailing tens of thousands of its members (Smith 1987, 72). When the Cuban civilian population was informed by Castro that the invasion force included former officials of the despised Batista regime, moreover, its support for Brigade 2506 was forfeited.

The battle was over and lost within days. Virtually every one of the invaders was either killed or captured. It was not until December 23, 1962, that the prisoners were released in exchange for a ransom of $53 million worth of medicine and food (Szulc 1986, 616). The costs to the international prestige of the United States and its power to influence the future of democracy in Cuba were even higher. We failed miserably and were revealed to the world as hypocrites for resorting to measures whose use by other na-

tions we had long condemned. Moreover, our participation in the operation resulted in solidifying Castro's rule and moving him closer to communism and the Soviet Union (Blasier 1976, 202). As Castro later confessed,
"Our Marxist-Leninist party was really born at (the Bay of Pigs); from that
date on, socialism became cemented forever with the blood of our workers,
peasants, and students" (Castro quoted in Szulc 1986, 615).

What convinced Kennedy to undertake such a disastrous policy? Two of
his confidantes, Arthur Schlesinger, Jr., and Senator J. William Fulbright, as
well as Ambassador Philip Bonsal and his staff at the American embassy in
Havana had advised against it for reasons that would ultimately prove pro-
phetic. "To give this activity even covert support," Fulbright told Kennedy,
"is of a piece with the hypocrisy and cynicism for which the United States is
constantly denouncing the Soviet Union in the United Nations and elsewhere. This point will not be lost on the rest of the world—nor on our own
consciences" (Fulbright quoted in Schlesinger 1967, 236). Schlesinger's
view was that Cuba did not present "so grave and compelling a threat to
our national security as to justify a course of action which much of the
world will interpret as calculated aggression against a small nation in defi-
ance both of treaty obligations and of the international standards as we
have repeatedly asserted against the Communist world" (238).

Ambassador Bonsal and his staff offered the following recommendation:

> The perception among the minority of Cuban people who tended to
> be anti-Castro was that the internal opposition to Castro was progres-
> sive and democratic, while the opposition in exile was made up in
> large part of former Batista supporters and was controlled by the
> CIA. Hence, while the introduction of a force from the outside had
> worked in Guatemala, it would almost certainly backfire in Cuba.
>
> Our best hope was to ride with the forces for change released by
> Castro himself, but to channel them in a direction less ideological and
> less antagonistic to enlightened U.S. interests. That meant that in the
> limited ways open to us, we ought to encourage the internal opposi-
> tion, which wanted reforms within a democratic system and without
> any ties to the Soviet Union. . . . In no event should we be perceived as
> intervening with force to turn back the clock and undo the popular re-
> forms Castro had instituted. (Smith 1987, 62–63)

Yet Kennedy would not be deterred. Many scholars, including
Schlesinger himself, conclude that he opposed the invasion but became "a
prisoner of events" set into motion by Eisenhower, the CIA, and the State
Department (Schlesinger 1967, 240). Others consider this explanation to be
"patent nonsense" (Ambrose 1993, 174). They argue that the tragedy at the

Bay of Pigs represented a marriage of pragmatism with the cold war anti-Communist mentality that Kennedy had displayed throughout his political career. During the 1960 presidential campaign, but prior to finding out about Brigade 2506, Kennedy endorsed at least in theory some sort of operation involving an attempted U.S. overthrow of Castro. "We must let the Cuban people know that we are sympathetic with their legitimate economic aspirations, that we are aware of their love for freedom, and that we will not be content until democracy is returned to Cuba," he said on September 23. "The forces fighting for freedom in exile and in the mountains of Cuba should be sustained and assisted" (Kennedy quoted in Blasier 1976, 201).

There was the further consequence of driving Cuba closer to the Soviet Union. Fearing additional CIA-induced coups, Castro requested help from Soviet Premier Nikita Khrushchev, who was more than happy to comply. Among the arms Khrushchev sent Castro were intermediate-range nuclear ballistic missiles and the equipment necessary to launch them. Although Kennedy had warned him against placing such weapons in Cuba, Khrushchev saw this as an opportunity to offset American nuclear missiles close to his own borders in Turkey. He also was unimpressed by Kennedy's waffling during the Bay of Pigs invasion and consequently did not take his warnings too seriously.

In order to demonstrate to Khrushchev his toughness and determination to preserve the sphere of influence in Latin America that the Monroe Doctrine historically had claimed for the United States, Kennedy took the radical step on October 22, 1962, of establishing an air and sea blockade of Cuba and placing American military forces on full alert for war. The world watched in horror as Soviet ships approached the 500-mile boundary Kennedy had set, fully expecting that their arrival would precipitate what has been called "the most serious crisis in the history of mankind" (Ambrose 1993, 182). At the very last moment Khrushchev backed down, recalled his ships, and entered into an agreement with Kennedy that the Soviets would take the missiles out of Cuba in return for pledges from the United States that it would cancel the blockade, remove its own nuclear weapons from Turkey, and not attack Castro.

According to Theodore Sorensen, one of the president's principal advisors, Kennedy's performance during the Cuban Missile Crisis constituted "his greatest success" in office (Sorensen 1966, 808). To Schlesinger, his performance "displayed the ripening of an American leadership unsurpassed in the responsible management of power" (Schlesinger 1967, 767). Yet the fact is that Kennedy's effectiveness in Cuba in 1962 never would have taken place without his pragmatic miscalculations there in 1961. As Tad Szulc, who witnessed these events as a *New York Times* correspondent in Havana, reported, "Unquestionably the Bay of Pigs affair led directly to the Cuban Missile Crisis in 1962" (Szulc 1986, 614).

BILL CLINTON AND GAYS IN THE MILITARY

While campaigning for president in October 1991 Bill Clinton not only pledged to end the ban on homosexuals in the armed services, which had existed since Congress created the Uniform Code of Military Justice in 1950, but promised to do it as one of the first acts of his administration. Why he made these pledges is not clear. Was it a matter of conscience? Was he courting the support of the homosexual community? Whatever his reason or reasons, Clinton was dubbed by homosexuals as the Abraham Lincoln of their civil rights movement and collected $3.5 million from gay and lesbian campaign contributors. It is estimated, moreover, that homosexuals cast one out of every seven votes Clinton received during the 1992 presidential election (Drew 1994, 42–43).

After being inaugurated, Clinton restated his determination to end the ban. Once again his motivation and judgment came under intense scrutiny. Why would he insist on keeping this particular promise when he had reneged on another campaign pledge to cut taxes for the middle class, a group whose support was potentially much more valuable to him? Why would he focus on the issue of homosexuals in the armed services when the United States faced other serious political, social, and economic problems? Why would he risk angering the military when they already suspected him of being a Vietnam-era draft dodger who wanted to slash their budget?

Clinton's logic by itself was clear enough. The Fifth Amendment's due process clause declares that no person shall "be deprived of life, liberty, or property, without due process of law." The equal protection clause of the Fourteenth Amendment prohibits a state from denying "to any person within its jurisdiction the equal protection of the laws." Taken together these amendments mean that governments cannot discriminate against what the United States Supreme Court has referred to as "suspect classifications" of Americans. In *United States v. Carolene Products Co.* Justice Harlan Fiske Stone defined suspect classes as "discrete and insular minorities" who have been deliberately and unreasonably mistreated by governments in the past (304 U.S. 154 [1938]). In *San Antonio School District v. Rodriguez* Justice Lewis Powell argued that "the traditional indicia of suspectness include a class saddled with such disabilities, or subjected to such a history of purposeful unequal treatment, or relegated to such a position of political powerlessness as to command extraordinary protection from the majoritarian political process" (411 U.S. 22–3 [1972]).

Of course, governments could not function if the law did not allow them to make some distinctions between people. Minimum qualifications can thus be established for citizenship as well as for such activities as voting and driving. As a general rule, however, the Constitution requires that governments base their distinctions on conduct, not status (Burns, Peltason, et al. 1998, 121). Traditionally, this is what Americans have meant by equality of opportunity: the idea that it is not who you are that counts, but what you do, and the expectation that we will be defined by nothing other than the content of our character. This also is what Martin Luther King, Jr., dreamed in 1963. In recognition of that dream, Bill Clinton said during the 1992 presidential campaign:

> We live in a country where we need the skill and abilities and contributions of everyone. It's an indisputable fact that a certain percentage of our fellow citizens are gay and lesbian. As long as they obey the law and don't do things to other people that they shouldn't do, they—just like other citizens—ought to have the right to work and serve in the military and to function in our country. The real issue is not whether you are gay or not but whether you can own up to being gay and still have your job or still serve your country. (Clinton quoted in Bull 1993, 40–41)

In fact homosexuals have fought in every war, sometimes with distinction. Some of the greatest military strategists, including Julius Caesar, Alexander the Great, and Frederick the Great, were either gay or bisexual. Among the countries that currently permit homosexuals to serve in the military are Australia, Canada, Denmark, France, Germany, Israel, Italy, Japan, the Netherlands, Norway, and Spain (Duffy 1993, 16). In recognition of these facts, and consistent with the United States Constitution, Clinton recommended just weeks into his presidency in January 1993 that sexual orientation per se should no longer be a precondition for service in the U.S. armed forces.

Despite the logic and historical accuracy of Clinton's proposal, it provoked fierce opposition from the population at large, Congress, and the military establishment. Fearful that the controversy would reduce his political capital and threaten his popular appeal, Clinton called for a six-month cooling-off period during which time, he hoped, a rapprochement could be worked out. In the meantime, he ordered the military to stop asking recruits about their sexual orientation and refrain from investigating charges that personnel were homosexual. As a concession to his adversaries, nevertheless, he permitted the armed services to transfer openly gay and lesbian personnel to the standby reserve, where they would forfeit both their pay and benefits (Bostdorff 1996, 197).

Leading the opposition were General Colin Powell, chair of the Joint Chiefs of Staff, and Sam Nunn, chair of the Senate Armed Services Committee. They expressed concern that Clinton's plan would interfere with combat effectiveness by weakening troop morale and by undermining the American military culture where privacy does not exist and a very high premium is placed on group cohesion and mutual trust. They also feared that ending the ban would scare away prospective recruits, cause devoutly religious personnel to resign, and increase the incidence of AIDS within the ranks. To dramatize his concerns Nunn staged a news event meant to illustrate the close quarters sailors must endure on navy ships and threatened to translate the Uniform Code of Military Justice into statute law, where it would be harder for Clinton to change it (198).

Six months later on July 19, 1993, Clinton issued an executive order establishing a "Don't ask, don't tell, don't pursue" policy that was far different from the program he had endorsed while campaigning and at the beginning of his administration. According to the new requirements, Americans can neither be blocked from joining the military nor discharged because of their homosexual status. Moreover, the military is prohibited from asking volunteers to disclose their sexual orientation and discouraged from investigating the sexual activities of enlisted personnel. On the other hand, personnel can be dismissed for publicly proclaiming their homosexuality or for openly engaging in homosexual acts while on- and off-duty. Clinton's order defines a homosexual act as "any bodily contact, actively undertaken or passively permitted, between members of the same sex for the purpose of satisfying sexual desires or any bodily contact which a reasonable person would understand to demonstrate a propensity or intent to engage in homosexual acts" (Aspin 1993, 2).

In other words, at the same time that Clinton's policy posits a contradiction between homosexuality and military service in theory, it permits homosexuals to serve in practice as long as they are discreet about their behavior. For personnel who openly identify themselves as gay or lesbian, it also creates a "rebuttable presumption" that they are not engaging in the kind of physical acts that distinguish homosexual sex from heterosexual sex in the first place. Clinton called these new requirements an "honorable compromise" with his original intentions to rule out sexual orientation as a relevant factor for military service and make disruptive behavior, including sexual harassment of any kind, the only acceptable justification for dismissal (Towell 1993a, 1970).

Neither friends nor foes of ending the ban shared Clinton's optimism. Gay rights advocates felt betrayed. "Once again, we have seen our dreams and our hopes for freedom sacrificed upon the altar of expediency," claimed David Mixner, a Clinton political adviser (1966). Social conservatives characterized the policy as insincere and inconsistent. "We're saying you can be a homosexual, but you can't act like a homosexual," observed Daniel Coats, a Republican member of the Senate Armed Services Committee (1969). Journalist Michael Kramer described it as "morally reprehensible, a first-ever official codification of a policy that encourages concealing a fact deemed material to an institution's smooth functioning" (Kramer 1993, 41).

However else "Don't ask, don't tell, don't pursue" may be interpreted, it represents the epitome of pragmatic political leadership. Clinton began by asserting the traditional American principle of equality of opportunity and by reminding us that we do not have to be fans of the homosexual lifestyle to defend that principle. It will be remembered that Abraham Lincoln held many prejudicial opinions about African Americans even as he maintained the absolute immorality of slavery. When Clinton was finished with this particular issue, however, he had trivialized equal opportunity. Sexual harassment is unacceptable in any culture, whether military or civilian. But what about sexual orientation? Either it is relevant to the military or it is not. Prudent leaders cannot have it both ways. As United States Appellate Judge Abner Mikva explained, "the government cannot discriminate in an effort to avoid the effects of others' prejudices. There is no 'military exception' to the Constitution" (Mikva quoted in Towell 1993b, 3211). And as former senator and presidential nominee Barry Goldwater remarked just before he passed away, "You don't need to be 'straight' to fight and die for your country. You just need to shoot straight" (Goldwater quoted in Burns, Peltason, et al. 1998, 575).

Clinton could have applied different strategies to this issue. Instead of springing gay rights on the country at the very beginning of his first term, Clinton could have prudently planned to wait until he had accumulated some political capital and gained the confidence of groups such as the military establishment and middle-class voters by championing laws and policies that served their interests. At that time he could have planned to ask these groups to repay him by going along with his original proposal to extend full-fledged equality of opportunity to gays in the armed services. Or Clinton could have idealistically insisted on full-fledged equality of opportunity for gays in the armed services from the start and refused to make any concessions to his critics. Or he could have cynically promised to support gays during his 1992 presidential campaign in return for contributions and votes and then abandoned them once he took office and the controversy over homosexuality became too hot for him to handle.

Other examples of pragmatic presidential policies include FDR's attitude toward African Americans and European Jews, Eisenhower's approach to school desegregation, and George Bush's positions on child care and environmental protection (Koenig 1996, 298). In all of these instances presidents displayed the traits that distinguish pragmatic leaders from prudent ones. Whereas leaders, consciously or unconsciously following the paradigm of Aristotelian prudence, emphasize moral ideals over tangible end results, pragmatists emphasize the tangible end results. Truman desperately wanted World War II to end and paid more attention to finding a "quick fix" to the problem than worrying about the long-term consequences of using the atomic bomb. Rather than openly challenge the powerful demagogue Joseph McCarthy and run the risk of losing some measure of public approval, Eisenhower chose to restrict his opposition to behind-the-scenes tactics. Kennedy tried to avoid confronting the moral implications of a cynical CIA-inspired plot to invade Cuba and overthrow Castro by settling for a compromise between what the CIA proposed and calling the operation off. Clinton was willing to compromise the fundamental American ideal of equality under the law for fear that continuing to support authentic equal opportunity for gays in the military would interfere with other aspects of his political agenda.

Conclusion

As the previous analysis appears to reveal, when presidents have been successful, they have followed the prescriptions of prudence, just as Aristotle predicted thousands of years ago. Consciously or unconsciously they strove to master politics by reconciling universal ideals and material circumstances, that is, by simultaneously "working out human good in specific contexts" (Moskop 1996, 631) and working to see that "the highest things come alive in human action" (Cochran 1991, 52). In Aristotle's own words, they sought to "make good shots at some attainable advantage" (Aristotle 1966, 631). They endeavored, moreover, to strike a balance between what Reinhold Niebuhr calls "the wisdom of the serpent and the harmlessness of the dove" in order to "beguile, deflect, harness and restrain self-interest, individual and collective, for the sake of the community" (Niebuhr 1944, 40–41).

Since they believed that selfishness is neither easy to control nor easily translated into the public interest, presidents fashioning successful policies rejected idealism and operated on the basis of the tragic conclusion that evil is an inherent part of politics. Unlike cynics and pragmatists, however, they refused either to resign themselves to evil or abandon moral goals for the sake of expediency. Instead they elected to do their very best to find solutions to insolvable problems through a form of politics that Niebuhr portrays as a convergence of conscience and power: "where the ethical and coercive factors of human life . . . interpenetrate and work out their tentative and uneasy compromises" (Niebuhr 1932, 4).

When presidents have succeeded, indeed, they always were willing to compromise, but never for the sake of compromise itself. They understood that their effectiveness would depend on intuition and luck as well as on reason. In addition, they were able to create policies for the present that arise out of the context of the American past while preparing the United States for the future. In the process they made every effort to keep doctrinaire ideologies and dogmas from interfering with their creativity and obstructing their vision. During the Civil War, historian T. Harry Williams writes, Abraham Lincoln

> would not have been able to comprehend the attempts of modern writers to classify his ideas into an ideology. Indeed, he would not have known what an ideology was. Although he believed deeply in certain principles which might be called his philosophy of politics, those principles were at the opposite pole of what is termed ideology today. . . . Lincoln distrusted deep theoretical thinkers and their slick assurance that they knew what the world needed. He was too conscious of the realities in every situation to be an ideologue. One of the keys to his thinking is his statement that few things in the world were wholly good or wholly evil. . . . As somebody has remarked, Lincoln was not the kind of man who is ready to do what God would do if God had all the facts. (Williams 1953, 96–97)

Lincoln is the president who probably comes closest to meeting Aristotle's paradigm of prudent political leadership. Although he never served as president, General George Marshall is another American who approaches Aristotle's ideal. Marshall's decision-making style involved solving a problem by imagining its multifaceted dimensions. In his preference for an English Channel invasion of Nazi-dominated Europe over a plan favored by the English to attack on the Eastern Mediterranean front, for instance, he considered not only military factors but relevant moral, political, social, and economic ones as well (Acheson 1969, 141). According to his successor as secretary of state, Dean Acheson, Marshall was truly a "Man for All Seasons" (142), who personified "the essence and the method—or rather the art—of judgment in its highest form . . . which requires both mastery of precise information and apprehension of imponderables" (141). To Acheson, it was only by "an act of God" that the United States was able to benefit from Marshall's prudence during the turbulent years of World War II and the Cold War.

The prudent policies that Lincoln and Marshall often created and per-suaded their countrymen and -women to accept entitle them to member-ship in that exalted group of leaders known as statesmen. "A Statesman," Edmund Burke maintains:

> differs from a professor in an university; the latter has only the gen-eral view of society; the former, the statesman, has a number of cir-cumstances to combine with those general ideas, and to take into his consideration. Circumstances are infinite, are infinitely combined; are variable and transient; he who does not take them into consideration is not erroneous, but stark mad . . . he is metaphysically mad. A states-man, never losing sight of principles, is to be guided by circum-stances; and, judging contrary to the exigencies of the moment, he may ruin his country forever. (Burke quoted in Morgenthau 1967, 220)

In view of the apparent connection between Aristotelian prudence and successful presidential leadership, it might be expected that the concept would play a significant role in contemporary studies of the office and pres-idents who often acted prudently. In fact this is not the case at all. Usually it is totally ignored. And when, on those rare occasions prudence does appear in contemporary presidential studies, it frequently has undergone a radical redefinition. In contrast to the dynamic visionary quality originally im-parted to it by Aristotle, today it seems to emphasize nothing more than "caution, a special regard for one's personal interests, and a pragmatic ap-proach to life" (Bill 1997, 203).

This tendency to confuse what Aristotle means by *phronesis* with the rather passive defense of moral principles found in pragmatism, or *prudentia*, reached comic proportions during the presidency of George Bush. While in office, Bush was unmercifully mimicked and teased on television shows such as *Saturday Night Live* for his frequent use of the phrase "Wouldn't be prudent!" Bush would employ this catch phrase to account for why his policies often simply "split the difference" (Koenig 1996, 298) between competing points of view, causing his policies to lack what he deri-sively referred to as "the vision thing."

Among presidential scholars the abandonment of prudence and/or its misidentification with pragmatism can be illustrated by an overview of the current literature. The relative merits of Richard Neustadt's, James David Barber's and George C. Edwards III's influential scholarship were debated in the Introduction. While these authors apparently consider Aristotle to be irrelevant to the study of the presidency, nothing they have written directly violates his political philosophy. Presidents are not imprudent merely because they strive to become more persuasive, love their work, and attempt to translate public approval into a successful legislative program.

The problem lies with what the scholarship of Neustadt, Barber, and Edwards omits. Since they are unable to tell us much about the ethical purposes of political power, their analyses of presidential leadership are flawed and incomplete. These flaws are especially meaningful at the present time when the institution of the presidency is in crisis over the very issue of moral leadership.

Although Neustadt, Barber, and Edwards totally ignore Aristotelian prudence, they consider FDR, one of the most prudent presidents, to be a model of presidential leadership. "No modern President has been more nearly master in the White House," Neustadt writes (Neustadt 1980, 118–19). Despite the chaotic political situation that confronted him when he assumed office, Barber argues, FDR's active-positive character guaranteed that he would take charge of it (Barber 1992, 295). Edwards describes FDR's first "hundred days" in office as one of "the most prolific periods of presidential legislative success" (Edwards 1989, 170). Another influential presidential scholar who admires FDR's politics on the whole, but disregards the prudential nature of his leadership, is James MacGregor Burns. FDR believed "that government could be used as a means to human betterment," Burns maintains. "He preached the need to make government efficient and honest. He wanted to help the underdog, although not necessarily at the expense of the top dog. He believed that private, special interests must be subordinated to the general interest. He sought to conserve both the national resources and the moral values of America" (Burns 1956, 155).

Nevertheless, Burns criticizes FDR for lacking a unified philosophic basis for his beliefs and deeds. His "mind was an eminently operative one, quick, keen, fact flexible," Burns writes. "It showed in his intellectual habits. He disdained elaborate, fine-spun theories. . . . He hated abstractions. His mind yearned for the detail, the particular, the specific. . . . He had a passion for the concrete" (334). Burns further charges that FDR's untheoretical turn of mind clouded his judgment and led him to develop a Machiavellian split personality involving a "derangement of ends and means" (Burns 1970, 609). One of FDR's separate personalities, Burns argues, was dedicated to the realization of transcendent ideals; the other to the acquisition of political power for its own sake.

From the perspective of prudent leadership, Burns's criticism must be taken very seriously because Aristotle insists that effective leadership requires that political ends and means be commensurate. Of course this assumes that his analogy between Machiavelli and FDR is valid, which it is not. In fact, Machiavelli's political philosophy does not contain incompatible goals and methods. In *The Prince*, which Burns frequently cites, Machiavelli dismisses universal ideals with the statement, "there's such a difference between the way we really live and the way we ought to live that the man who neglects the real to study the ideal will learn how to accomplish his ruin, not his salvation" (Machiavelli 1992, 42). Having thus represented ideals such as the common good to be an unrealistic primary goal for rulers to pursue, Machiavelli further encourages them to use whatever strategy, moral or immoral, that is necessary to further their own interests. "In the actions of all men, and especially of princes who are not subject to a court of appeal," he claims, "we must always look to the end" (49). For Machiavelli, in other words, the end of gaining and maintaining political power justifies the means rulers efficiently utilize to realize that end.

Machiavelli also advises princes to "pick for imitation the fox and the lion. As a lion cannot protect himself from traps, and the fox cannot defend himself from wolves, you have to be a fox in order to be wary of traps, and a lion to overawe the wolves. Those who try to live by the lion alone are badly mistaken" (48). His metaphor is instructive: by positing the behavior of lions and foxes as something human beings should emulate, Machiavelli demonstrates that there is nothing inconsistent about his unabashed cynicism. As he fully comprehends, lions and foxes possess neither souls nor the ability to pursue moral goals.

Nor, for the most part, were FDR's ends and means incommensurate. On the whole his political career reflected thoroughgoing commitments to "humane and democratic values" and to "better the life of the average American" (Goodwin 1994, 630). His genius lay in combining the conscience of a decent man with the vision of an extraordinarily creative artist and the cunning of a master politician into a prudent whole that was greater than the sum of its parts (Sherwood 1950, 73). Even when he made such notable mistakes as signing the Japanese Exclusion Act and treating African Americans and European Jews unjustly, his errors were generally caused by cynical and pragmatic deviations from Aristotelian prudence, not an inconsistency between goals and methods.

Excluding the Japanese from the West Coast was a downright cynical act. His attitude toward African Americans and European Jews was pragmatic. He did just enough to help them, but not enough to do much good. He outlawed racial discrimination in the federal government and defense industries, but was unwilling to support Senator Robert Wagner's anti-lynching bill and refused to desegregate the armed services. He allowed 105,000 European Jews to immigrate to the United States (Goodwin 1994, 101), but denied entrance to millions more who were desperate to flee for their lives. He also refused to bomb either the rail lines transporting Jews and others to the gas chambers or the death camps themselves. FDR rationalized these pragmatic decisions by claiming that he could not afford to lose the support of racist members of Congress for his New Deal reforms.

On the other hand, FDR's scheme to pack the United States Supreme Court in 1937, for which he was almost unanimously denounced, does conform more closely to Burns's criticism. Frustrated by a majority of the court's laissez-faire approach to public policy, he sought at the beginning of his second term to appoint an additional justice committed to the New Deal for every federal court judge aged seventy or over. This would have allowed him to add a maximum of six new members to the Supreme Court and forty-four new lower federal court judges. As Burns correctly points out, FDR's scheme was an ill-advised and ill-designed attempt to increase his power to protect constitutional rights by tampering with the constitutional principle of separation of powers.

FDR's "main trouble was intellectual," Burns concludes (Burns 1956, 334). His thesis is that FDR's distrust of abstractions, attributed by Burns to what the famed jurist Oliver Wendell Holmes called his "second class intellect" (147), made it impossible for him to appreciate the proper relationship between means and ends. Yet Aristotle teaches that there are two different forms of reason: theoretical, dealing solely with abstractions; and practical, seeking to reconcile abstractions with material circumstances. In Aristotle's view theoretical reason may apply well to metaphysics and mathematics, but only its practical counterpart is capable of coping successfully with the complex issues confronted by flesh and blood human beings living in organic political communities. Despite Burns's and Holmes's charges, the evidence suggests that, while FDR was not an ideologue, he did believe in the intrinsic value of such universal ideals as the Golden Rule and the Ten Commandments and for the most part dedicated his presidency to translating them into public policy.

The relationship of Aristotelian prudence to the presidencies of Washington and Lincoln has also often been missed. Historian Edmund Morgan describes the role Washington played in the nation's founding as primarily that of a shrewd practitioner of power politics. His main talent, Morgan writes, "lay in his understanding of power . . . an understanding unmatched by that of his contemporaries" (Morgan 1980, 6). But Morgan's portrayal deemphasizes the essential moral character of Washington's leadership. Shrewd practitioners of power politics generally are cynics who exploit and manipulate people for their own purposes. Washington's politics, however, was limited by the just ends he attempted to achieve. Aristotle reminds us that "it is not possible to be (prudent) in the true sense of the word without . . . virtue" (Aristotle 1966, 191). As Pierce Butler, one of the delegates to the 1787 Philadelphia Constitutional Convention, similarly observed: "I do (not) believe they (the executive powers) would have been so great had not many members cast their eyes toward George Washington as president; and shaped their ideas of the powers to be given the president, by their opionion of his virtue" (Butler quoted in Koenig 1996, 31).

In his important two-volume study, *Lincoln the President*, historian J. G. Randall depicts him as a cynic who was not above using half-truths to win elections and remain in office. As we know, Lincoln opposed Stephen Douglas's proposal to allow local plebiscites to decide the fate of slavery in the territories. Randall considers Lincoln's case against Douglas—that popular sovereignty does not extend to denying another person's humanity—to be hollow and essentially unsubstantive. Since Lincoln knew that the history and geography of most of the territories were not conducive to a slave economy, Randall argues, he could give the false impression of being principled and gain votes from a variety of factions in the process. It is also Randall's contention that since Douglas, Lincoln's main opponent in the 1858 Illinois senatorial and 1860 presidential elections, also was aware of these unfavorable conditions, it "would be a perversion of history" to take the "difference between the two men "seriously (Randall 1945, 1: 127).

Assuming that popular sovereignty would have led to the same result in the territories that Lincoln favored, does it really make sense to so thoroughly disparage his logic and motives? Is it really a half-truth to claim that popular sovereignty is not an end in itself, but a means to the end of political justice? Lincoln believed in democracy and certainly wanted to win elections but was willing to risk his political fortunes on the conviction that it would be unconscionable to allow an evil institution to spread to places in the United States where it had not already been established. As political scientist Leo Strauss observes, "the true statesman in the Aristotelian sense . . . takes his bearings" from the view that "there is a universally valid hierarchy of ends, but there are no universally valid rules of action. . . . [W]hen deciding what ought to be done, i.e., what ought to be done by this individual (or this individual group) here and now, one has to consider not only which of the various competing objectives is higher in rank but also which is most urgent in the circumstances" (Strauss 1965, 162).

Historian Richard Hofstadter's analysis of Lincoln concentrates on his political ambition, what Lincoln's friend and law partner William Herndon called "a little engine that knew no rest" (Hofstadter 1961, 93). Hofstadter argues that Lincoln was what today would be called an expert "spin doctor," a public relations guru, who originated the mythology that continues to place him among history's foremost statesmen and has elevated him to the level of "the greatest character since Christ" (93). In fact, Hofstadter maintains, he was less like a demigod than a demagogue as well as a "deliberate and responsible" opportunist (97); a courtier of "influential and financial friends" (100); a world-class "political propagandist" (111); a "professional politician looking for votes" (116); and a "follower . . . not a leader of public opinion" (133). The Emancipation Proclamation, Hofstadter adds, has "all the moral grandeur of a bill of lading" (132).

What would cause Hofstadter to paint such an unflattering portrait? We know that no one gets to be president of this country without being ambitious. The key question is what a president does after assuming office. Lincoln's presidency led to the preservation of the Union, along with its ideals, and the eventual passage of the Thirteenth, Fourteenth, and Fifteenth amendments. Although historian Richard Current does not refer to Aristotelian prudence when describing Lincoln, he fortunately offers a necessary corrective to Hofstadter's exaggerated interpretation. Lincoln "has been described as essentially a politician's politician, as a pragmatist, a man more interested in immediate, practical advantages than in underlying principles," Current writes:

> He has been characterized as a flexible man rather than one of fixed determination. In fact, however, he was flexible and pragmatic only in his choice of means and in his sense of timing. Though no doctrinaire, Lincoln was a man of deep conviction and settled purpose. Only by compromising with the necessities of his time could he hope to gain and hold political power. And only by holding political power could he hope to give reality, even in part, to his concept of the Union and its potentialities. (Current 1967, xxix)

Among the historians who have misidentified prudence as pragmatism in their analyses of presidents who have fashioned successful policies are David Donald, Arthur Schlesinger, Jr., and Robert Dallek. While pragmatism does not deny ideals, it remains dedicated to tangible results and therefore is more apt than prudence to compromise principles for the sake of political power. In *Lincoln Reconsidered* Donald describes him in prudential terms as a president who "possessed what John Keats called the 'quality [that] went to form a Man of Achievement,' that quality 'which Shakespeare possessed so enormously— . . . *Negative Capability*, that is when a man is capable of being in uncertainties, Mysteries, doubts, without any irritable reaching after fact and reason.' " (Donald 1961, 143). Then Donald confuses the issue by locating Lincoln within what he identifies as "the American pragmatic tradition" (1961, 128). He repeats the mistake in his more recent *Lincoln* where he cites Lincoln's "pragmatic approach to problems" (Donald 1995, 15).

In his monumental three-volume *The Age of Roosevelt* Schlesinger celebrates FDR's "ability to stir idealism in people's souls" (Schlesinger 1958,
544). He seconds the observation of Harry Hopkins, one of FDR's closest
advisors, that he was "a great spiritual figure" (585). And he argues that "at
bottom" FDR "had a guiding vision with substantive content of its own"
(Schlesinger 1960, 652). Although these qualities help to define a prudent
leader, Schlesinger insists on classifying FDR as "the eternal pragmatist"
(Schlesinger 1958, 257), who "had no philosophy save experiment"
(Schlesinger 1960, 654). He describes the New Deal, moreover, as a policy of
"trial and error pragmatism" (155) whose strengths were "that it had no
doctrine, that it was improvised and opportunistic, that it was guided only
by circumstance" (654).

The problem with Schlesinger's analysis is that, whatever else they may
have to offer, pragmatists are people whose businesslike practicality and
emphasis on material rewards prevent them from either becoming "spiritual figures" or stirring "idealism in people's souls." A similar contradiction marks Dallek's work. The author of an acclaimed biography of Lyndon
Johnson, Dallek prudently observes that "the men who have survived and
prospered in the White House have been those with the keenest political
sense: presidents who combined a clear sense of purpose with both a carefully judged assessment of what degree of change the country was ready to
accept and a strategic sense of when to accommodate themselves to opponents who were ready to yield on at least some points" (Dallek 1996, 44). Yet
he incorrectly labels as pragmatic politics "practiced as an art, with a
pallette of just the right shades of principle, bravado, and compromise"
(45). Of Lincoln, Dallek argues that he "put practical politics in the service . . . of the country's highest ideals" (54). Nevertheless he later calls Lincoln "the great pragmatist" (55).

What's going on? Why does prudence continue to be neglected and misidentified by esteemed presidential scholars? The problem appears to lie
not with the concept, that seems to be an obvious political talent most presidents would want to claim for themselves, but with the Aristotelian political philosophy upon which prudence is based. Indeed, there appears to
exist in American culture what political scientist Allan Bloom calls a "contempt" for Aristotle (Bloom 1987, 311) that can be traced back to his positions on reality, human nature, freedom, and democracy.

Aristotle's view of reality emphasizes immaterial transcendent ideals,
but not to the exclusion of material circumstances. His prudent leaders thus
seek to harmonize the abstract public interest of a particular society with
the concrete selfish interests of that society's citizens. As political scientist
Michael Sandel observes: "Public policy is not a sovereign subject but a

subfield of political theory. No government official or policy analyst, however expert, has yet devised a way of resolving public questions without relying on a theory of the public interest" (Sandel 1988, 110). Yet, as Sandel further points out, Americans appear to be especially uncomfortable with such abstractions. Our concern is that government officials will palm off their own interpretations of what constitutes the public interest on us.

In his influential *The Governmental Process* David Truman speaks for mainstream political scientists in the United States when he contends that, in describing American politics, "we do not need to account for a totally inclusive interest, because one does not exist" (Truman 1971, 51). The assertion "that there is an interest of the nation as a whole, universally and invariably held and standing apart from and superior to those of the various groups included within it," Truman maintains, "flies in the face of all we know of the behavior of men in a complex society" (50).

Aristotle's accent on universal ideals underlies his search for enduring principles by which individuals can lead decent lives and governments can initiate some degree of justice in society. Nevertheless Americans appear to be very suspicious about universal ideals, fearing they will be appropriated by tyrants and become the source of dogmatic intolerance. "The tendency to abstract the principles of political life may sharpen issues for the political philosopher," historian Daniel Boorstin observes in *The Genius of American Politics*. "It becomes idolatry when it provides statesmen or a people with a blueprint for their society. The characteristic tyrannies of our age—naziism [*sic*], fascism, and communism—have expressed precisely this idolatry. They justify their outrages because their 'philosophies' require them" (Boorstin 1967, 3).

Consistent with his view of reality Aristotle believes that human beings are composed of a material body, the source of our animal appetites, and an immaterial soul, the power to choose between good and evil that distinguishes us from all other living things. While Aristotle is not a cynic because he never gives up hope that we will make moral choices, he lacks confidence in the power of our souls to control the bodily appetites and thus holds a relatively pessimistic view of human nature. According to Niebuhr, however, Americans tend to be much more sanguine about "the human capacity for transcendence over self-interest" (Niebuhr 1944, 39). "Our modern civilization," he explains, "was ushered in on a wave of boundless social optimism" (16).

Americans have displayed this optimism ever since the days of the Massachusetts Puritans when we set about creating "God's New Israel" in the New World. From then on the model American hero has been the rugged, self-sufficient individual who asks no quarter from and gives no quarter to anyone or anything: James Fenimore Cooper's frontiersman; Jefferson's small freehold farmer; Henry David Thoreau's civilly disobedient naturalist; Frederic Remington's cowboy; Horatio Alger's entrepreneurial capitalist; the "Lone Eagle," Charles Lindbergh; and the fabled Mercury astronauts. Even Lincoln is frequently remembered more for his "log cabin to the White House" exploits than for his prudential politics.

Aristotle's idea that the human soul is a two-edged sword leads to his definition of freedom. On the one hand, he argues, souls give us the power of free will. On the other hand, they require that we take full responsibility for our freely willed decisions. For Aristotle, therefore, authentic freedom is the product of a balance between our inclination to do as we please and our duty to act conscientiously. In *The Politics*, for instance, Aristotle defends the right to own private property but insists that it be utilized in a socially accountable manner. "The end for which the state exists," he writes, is the "quality of life," not just material possessions (Aristotle 1962, 118). Americans, however, tend to view freedom simply as the absence of coercion. Indeed, the traditional American attitude toward private property is that its ownership represents an unalienable, essentially unlimited, natural right. According to John Locke, the philosopher who arguably has had the greatest impact on American political thought, "the great and chief end . . . of men's uniting into commonwealths, and putting themselves under government, is the preservation of their property" (Locke 1974, 73).

When successful presidents are described in terms reminiscent of Aristotelian prudence, why are they often misidentified as pragmatists? Perhaps the reason is because pragmatism traditionally has been the philosophy of choice for most Americans. As was discussed in chapter 4, the framers of the Constitution all but gave up on establishing a political system directly and explicitly dedicated to the pursuit of political justice. Since it is impossible to convince Americans to sacrifice their short-term selfish interests for the long-term welfare of the United States, the framers concluded, the very best we can do is to create a government that actually encourages factionalism, tries to neutralize it by pitting factions against each other, and hopes that a parallelogram of forces will be produced that results in the public interest (Madison, Hamilton, and Jay 1961, 322).

In his highly regarded 1835 study, *Democracy in America*, Alexis de Tocqueville observes that "Americans have in a manner reduced egotism to a social and philosophical theory" (Tocqueville quoted in Bennett 1993, 181) and coins the phrase "the doctrine of self-interest properly understood" to describe the process by which Americans attempt to derive political justice from egotistic behavior, without challenging the validity of egotism itself. This doctrine, otherwise known as enlightened self-interest, appears to Tocqueville to be "the best suited of all philosophic theories to the wants of men in our time" (Tocqueville 1969, 527). As he notes:

> Self-interest properly understood is not at all a sublime doctrine, but it is clear and definite. It does not attempt to reach great aims, but it does, without too much trouble, achieve all it sets out to do. Being within the scope of everybody's understanding, everyone grasps it and has no trouble bearing it in mind. It is wonderfully ageeable to human weakness, and so easily wins great sway. It has no difficulty in keeping its power, for it turns private interest against itself and uses the same goad which excites them to direct passions. (526–27)

Despite our fear that metaphysical abstractions will be exploited and manipulated by tyrants for cynical purposes, the fact is that the two most frightening tyrannies of the twentieth century, Nazi Germany and Communist Russia, were based on a conspicuous rejection of universal ideals. Nazism is portrayed most accurately, in theologian Hermann Rauschning's words, as a "revolution of nihilism" in which every idea and principle is subverted by hatred and murder (Rauschning 1939, 24). Hitler thus championed National Socialism as an irrational "triumph of the will," where legitimacy is decided by power alone. Marxist-Leninist theory makes its position on transcendence clear. Through the doctrines of historical materialism and economic determinism it teaches that both history as a whole and specific epochs within history are controlled by advances in technology and fluctuations in the organization of labor. Truth for Marx and Lenin, consequently, is always relative to particular material conditions.

Of course, Aristotle is not an egalitarian and in the final analysis this factor may very well be the main reason we reject his political philosophy in general and ignore his theory of prudent political leadership in particular. We seem to fear that taking Aristotle seriously would be tantamount to accepting some dubious form of undemocratic, un-American elitism (Nussbaum 1994, 101). Yet, as political scientist John Hallowell reveals, free government is untenable unless democrats adhere to the universal ideals associated with Aristotle and the Western political tradition: "the absolute moral worth of the individual . . . the spiritual equality of individuals, and . . . the essential rationality of man" (Hallowell 1963, 80). "It is the belief in the absolute moral worth of the individual that prevents the individual from being submerged, if not obliterated, in a conception of the race, the class, the nation, or some other collectivity that regards the individual as a means rather than as an end in himself" (80–81), Hallowell maintains. He goes on to note:

It is in terms of the conception of the spiritual equality of individuals that we can understand the words in the Declaration of Independence that "all men are created equal" and strive toward the attainment of equality of opportunity for all men. . . . The phrase derived originally from the belief that all men are created equal in the sight of God, that the souls of men are equally precious to God, and that all individuals should be treated with the respect due to a creature made in the image and likeness of God. . . . God's image in man is reflected in the capacity of human beings to reason, and the disparagement of that capacity can lead only to the denial of man's uniqueness. (80–81)

Journalist Walter Lippmann makes a similar point. Contrary to popular opinion, he argues, democratic institutions cannot flourish in relativistic cultures where "all truths are self-centered and self-regarding, and all principles are the rationalization of some special interest" (Lippmann 1955, 114). Where "there is no public criterion of the true and the false, of the right and the wrong, beyond that which the preponderant mass of voters, consumers, readers and listeners happen at the moment to be supposed to want" (114), Lippmann asserts, "it is impossible to reach intelligible and workable conceptions of popular election, majority rule, representative assemblies, free speech, loyalty, property, corporations, and voluntary associations" (80).

Underlying all of Aristotle's thought is the assumption that ideas have consequences. This is another position that does not hold wide sway in the United States today. We appear to be very interested in how such factors as socioeconomic status, race, gender, age, religion, and nationality influence American politics. But on the influence of ideas, little is said. As Jeffrey Tulis remarks, we seem to believe "that ideas are 'epiphenomenal,' that is, mere reflections of important political developments" (Tulis 1987, 17). Let's face it, the ideal standards Aristotle sets for prudent leadership are so rigorous that few leaders have ever and will ever be able to meet them. Not even Lincoln, Washington, and FDR, the presidents most often identified by scholars for their greatness (Schlesinger 1996, 47), were unblemished in that regard. For this reason prudence has been characterized as "the 'intelligent prow' of our nature which steers through the multiplicity of the finite toward perfection" (Pieper 1959, 22).

By setting the standards so high, Aristotle hopes to stimulate as much effective political leadership as the circumstances will bear. Herein lies the danger to American government of holding Aristotle in contempt: the less we expect of our presidents, the less we are likely to get from them. Thomas Cronin has warned us about being blinded "to the limits of what a president can accomplish" by "an exaggerated sense of the possibilities of the

perfect, or what can be called our notion of the 'textbook presidency' "
(Cronin and Genovese 1998, 86). In his recent book on the Clinton impeachment, *An Affair of State*, Federal Circuit Court Judge Richard Posner maintains that one of the positive legacies of the proceedings is that it takes "the
President off his pedestal so that our politics can become perhaps more
pragmatic, less striving for some exalted notion of leadership" (Greenhouse 1999, 14). As if to confirm that we have taken Cronin's and Posner's
positions to heart, a September 1998 *New York Times/CBS News* poll reported
that, while only 21 percent of the public thought it important for presidents
to be moral role models, a full 63 percent approved of the way Clinton was
doing his job (Berke 1998, 1).

Political scientist John Pitney argues that this apparent contradiction in
the polling data can be explained by the historic tendency of American voters to identify with the sinner over the saint in order to justify our own im-
perfections. In the twentieth century, there probably was no president who
profited more from this tendency than Bill Clinton. From his dysfunctional
boyhood family experiences to his marijuana use, draft dodging, marital
discord, and sexual philandering, Clinton has made a career out of portraying his personal flaws to the electorate as strengths rather than weaknesses.
"People don't like perfection because they don't think it represents them,"
Pitney maintains. "Everybody has made missteps in his or her life and simply can relate to someone who has done like him. For people who like to be-
stow forgiveness, Bill Clinton is an absolute gift" (Pitney quoted in Tackett
2000, D4).

Fortunately, there are some exceptions to the rule. A few studies of spe-
cific presidents, the presidency, and modern executive leadership in general have incorporated Aristotelian prudence into their analyses. Harry
Jaffa's *Crisis of the House Divided*, treated in chapter 3, discovers profound
Aristotelian influences in Lincoln's ideas and behavior. Harvey Mansfield,
Jr.'s *Taming the Prince* traces the prejudice against Aristotle in the United
States to a form of Machiavellianism domesticated for use in American politics by the thought of Hobbes, Locke, and Montesquieu. Mansfield points
out that Aristotelian prudence enables leaders to utilize such means as reason, cunning, cleverness and a sense of common decency to combine "private interest with the common good by governing the virtues for the sake of
both" (Mansfield 1993, 209). According to Mansfield, however, "Machiavelli's
prudence is nothing but cunning, and his principality or republic (each of
which is a mixture of both), when prudently understood, inspires its
princes or citizens to abandon all loyalties impartially, save the one to themselves" (280).

By Mansfield's estimation, it is Machiavellian prudence, in a toned-down version suited to American tastes, that has been systematized in the United States. To the extent that his interpretation is accurate, indeed, whatever success presidents have enjoyed within this sytem in controlling their hunger for self-aggrandizement and fashioning policies that serve the public interest becomes all the more remarkable. To the extent that Mansfield's interpretation is accurate, moreover, it would tend to confirm Aristotle's confidence in the power of his own version of prudence to stimulate effective leadership. It is so powerful that, when properly employed by qualified chief executives, it can yield successful policies even in a cultural milieu antagonistic to many of its intellectual premises.

In *The President as Leader* political scientist Erwin Hargrove cites Shakespeare's Henry V as the paradigmatic Aristotelian leader who combines "power and virtue" into "effective rule" (Hargrove 1998, 20) and recognizes that "when prudence is forgotten, failure is guaranteed" (174). Effective rulers, Hargrove argues, possess the talent of "discernment" and are able to "teach reality" to their constituents. According to Hargrove, "teaching reality" involves "teaching what one understands to be moral truths" (45). "The prophets of the Bible were authentic figures to the community to which they preached because they appealed to the shared values of the faithful," he writes. "Presidents, at their best, do the same" (75). By Hargrove's definition, when Lincoln reminded us how essential equality of opportunity is to our culture and when Theodore Roosevelt insisted that we have a responsibility to preserve the environment for future generations, they were teaching reality to the American people.

Hargrove calls "discernment" the "master" leadership skill and describes it as the "ability to estimate, more or less accurately, the kinds of political action that will be successful in a given historical context" (35). When Washington convinced Americans that strong presidents do not necessarily have to become tyrants and Franklin Delano Roosevelt prepared the United States for the complex realities of the modern age that are no longer responsive to strict laissez-faire and isolationist policies, they were displaying what Hargrove terms discernment.

In *The Politics Presidents Make* political scientist Stephen Skowronek, without specifically referring to Aristotelian prudence, develops Hargrove's theme of discernment by attempting to understand presidential leadership within the dynamic framework of changing historical circumstances. Skowronek's position is that the kind of leadership that proves successful during a period of "reconstruction" (Skowronek 1993, 36), in which new political coalitions are developed, will not necessarily work during other periods when these coalitions are challenged and eventually overturned.

"Presidents are historical actors," Skowronek writes:

> Their words and deeds will transform the contexts in which they act,
> but they must act by their own lights within the context given. An old
> adage captures the point well: presidents, we say, want to secure *a
> place* in history. Echoes of *The Federalist Papers* ring clear here: presi-
> dents are driven by a concern for their reputation; they try to vindi-
> cate themselves in their stewardship of national affairs. But the old
> saying hints at something more: a president comes to power at a par-
> ticular moment in the course of national events, and vindication turns
> on the prospect for securing the meaning of *that* moment on the presi-
> dent's own terms. The question is, how do presidents go about the
> task of fashioning their places in history, and how amenable are these
> places to being fashioned according to presidential design? (18)

But these and other notable exceptions prove the rule. As Mansfield's
analysis indicates, the amoral Machiavellian power orientation continues
to prevail. Consequently, although none of the leading theories of the presidency appears to account for presidential behavior, including recent events
in the White House, as fully as Aristotle's theory of prudent political leadership, for the most part contemporary students of American politics have
ignored Aristotle. We seem to have concluded that, just because his ideas
are not fully reducible to the expectations of American culture, we are justified in dismissing everything he has to say.

We have now come full circle. One of the examples utilized in the second
chapter of this book to illustrate the meaning of Aristotelian prudence was
the Judeo-Christian principle of "love thy neighbor as thyself." When, in
the first century A.D., the legendary Jewish sage Hillel was asked to interpret
this principle, he said: "If I am not for myself, who will be for me? If I am
only for myself, what am I?" By the terms of Hillel's interpretation, the goal
of political justice can never be achieved unless decent people seek ways to
gain and maintain power for themselves. Once they are firmly established
in office and enjoy the perquisites of office, however, they are obliged to use
their influence to serve the public interest. The means they utilize, moreover, must be commensurate with the end they seek to achieve. That so
many scholars have found Hillel and Aristotle's forthright lessons to be un-
worthy of their research points to a source of confusion in the field of presidential studies. The fundamental goal of *The Prudential Presidency* is to
offset that confusion.

References

Abernathy, Thomas. 1968. *The Burr Conspiracy*. Gloucester, MA: Peter Smith.

Acheson, Dean. 1969. *Present at the Creation*. New York: W. W. Norton & Company.

Alperovitz, Gar. 1995. *The Decision to Use the Atomic Bomb*. New York: Alfred A. Knopf.

Ambrose, Stephen. 1993. *Rise to Globalism*. New York: Penguin Books.

———. 1989. *Nixon*. Volume 2. New York: Simon and Schuster.

———. 1984. *Eisenhower*. Volume 2. New York: Simon and Schuster.

Aristotle. 1966. *The Ethics*. Translated by J.A.K. Thomson. Baltimore: Penguin Books.

———. 1962. *The Politics*. Translated by Ernest Barker. New York: Oxford University Press.

Aspin, Les. 1993. *Memorandum to the Joint Chiefs of Staff*. Washington, DC: Government Printing Office.

Bailey, F. G. 1988. *Humbuggery and Manipulation: The Art of Leadership*. Ithaca, NY: Cornell University Press.

Baldwin, Hanson. 1950. *Great Mistakes of the War*. New York: Harper and Brothers.

Barber, James David. 1992. *The Presidential Character*. 4th ed. Englewood Cliffs, NJ: Prentice-Hall.

Beiner, Ronald. 1983. *Political Judgment*. London: Methuen.

Beloff, Max. 1965. *Thomas Jefferson and American Democracy*. New York: Collier Books.

Bennett, William. 1993. *The Book of Virtues*. New York: Simon and Schuster.

Berke, Richard. 1998. "In Presidents, Virtues Can Be Flaws (And Vice Versa)." *New York Times*, September 27. section 4, p. 4.

Bernstein, Carl, and Bob Woodward. 1974. *All the President's Men*. New York: Simon and Schuster.

Bessette, Joseph, and Jeffrey Tulis. 1981. "The Constitution, Politics, and the Presidency." In Joseph Bessette and Jeffrey Tulis, eds., *The Presidency in the Constitutional Order*, 3–30. Baton Rouge: Louisiana State University Press.

Bill, James. 1997. *George Ball: Behind the Scenes in U.S. Foreign Policy*. New Haven: Yale University Press.

Blasier, Cole. 1976. *The Hovering Giant*. Pittsburgh: University of Pittsburgh Press.

Bloom, Allan. 1987. *The Closing of the American Mind*. New York: Simon and Schuster.

Bluhm, William. 1965. *Theories of the Political System*. Englewood Cliffs, N.J: Prentice-Hall.

Blum, John. 1967. *The Republican Roosevelt*. Cambridge, MA: Harvard University Press.

———. 1956. *Woodrow Wilson and the Politics of Morality*. Boston: Little, Brown and Co.

Blum, John, Edmund Morgan, et al. 1977. *The National Experience*. New York: Harcourt Brace Jovanovich.

Boorstin, Daniel. 1967. *The Genius of American Politics*. Chicago: University of Chicago Press.

Bostdorff, Denise. 1996. "Clinton's Characteristic Issue Management Style: Caution, Conciliation, and Conflict Avoidance in the Case of Gays in the Military." In Robert Denton and Rachel Holloway, eds., *The Clinton Presidency*, 189–223. Westport, CT: Greenwood Press.

Bull, Chris. 1993. "And the Ban Played On." *The Advocate* (March): 37–43.

Burke, Edmund. 1955. *Reflections on the Revolution in France*. Edited by Thomas Mahoney. Indianapolis: Bobbs-Merrill.

Burnham, Walter Dean. 1997. "Bill Clinton: Riding the Tiger." In Gerald Pomper, ed., *The Election of 1996*, 1–20. Chatham, NJ: Chatham House.

Burns, James MacGregor. 1970. *Roosevelt: The Soldier of Freedom*. New York: Harcourt Brace Jovanovich.

———. 1956. *Roosevelt: The Lion and the Fox*. New York: Harcourt, Brace and World.

Burns, James MacGregor, J. W. Peltason, et al. 1998. *Government by the People*. Upper Saddle River, NJ: Prentice-Hall.
Canavan, Francis. 1960. *The Political Ideas of Edmund Burke*. Durham, NC: Duke University Press.
Carter, Jimmy. 1982. *Keeping the Faith: Memoirs of a President*. New York: Bantam Books.
Clark, Bennett Champ. 1932. *John Quincy Adams*. New York: Alfred A. Knopf.
Clements, Kendrick. 1992. *The Presidency of Woodrow Wilson*. Lawrence: University Press of Kansas.
Cochran, Clarke. 1991. "Aquinas, Prudence and Health Care Policy." In Ethan Fishman, ed., *Public Policy and the Public Good*, 47–62. Westport, CT: Greenwood Press.
The Commission on Wartime Relocation and Internment of Civilians. 1982. *Personal Justice Denied*. Washington, DC: Government Printing Office.
Corwin, Edwin. 1957. *The President: Office and Powers*. New York: New York University Press.
Cronin, Thomas, and Michael Genovese. 1998. *The Paradoxes of the American Presidency*. New York: Oxford University Press.
Curran, Eddie. 1999. "The Tobacco War's Home Front." *Mobile Register*, October 31, pp. 1, 24.
Current, Richard, ed. 1967. *The Political Thought of Abraham Lincoln*. Indianapolis: Bobbs-Merrill.
Cutright, Paul. 1956. *Theodore Roosevelt: The Naturalist*. New York: Harper and Brothers.
Dahl, Norman. 1984. *Practical Reason, Aristotle, and the Weakness of the Will*. Minneapolis: University of Minnesota Press.
Daley, Robert. 1978. *Prince of the City*. Boston: Houghton Mifflin.
Dallek, Robert. 1996. *Hail to the Chief*. New York: Hyperion.
Daniels, Roger. 1975. *The Decision to Relocate the Japanese Americans*. Philadelphia: J. B. Lippincott Co.
Dickinson, William. 1974. *Watergate: Chronology of a Crisis*. Volume 1. Washington, DC: Congressional Quarterly Inc.
Donald, David. 1995. *Lincoln*. New York: Simon and Schuster.
———. 1961. *Lincoln Reconsidered*. New York: Vintage Books.
Drew, Elizabeth. 1994. *On the Edge: The Clinton Presidency*. New York: Simon and Schuster.
Duffy, Brian, and Kenneth Walsh. 1998. "Solace Abroad, Trouble at Home." *U.S. News and World Report*, September 14, pp. 14–19.
Duffy, Michael. 1993. "Obstacle Course." *Time*. February 8, pp. 16, 26–28.
Dunne, Joseph. 1993. *Back to the Rough Ground: "Phronesis" and "Techne" in Modern Philosophy and in Aristotle*. Notre Dame: University of Notre Dame Press.

Edwards, George C., III. 1989. *At the Margins*. New Haven: Yale University Press.

———. 1983. "Quantitative Analysis." In George C. Edwards III and Stephen J. Wayne, eds., *Studying the Presidency*, 99–124. Knoxville: University of Tennessee Press.

———. 1980. *Presidential Influence in Congress*. San Francisco: Freeman.

Edwards, George C., III, and Stephen J. Wayne. 1999. *Presidential Leadership*. New York: Worth Publishers.

Ellis, Joseph. 1997. *American Sphinx: The Character of Thomas Jefferson*. New York: Knopf.

Fishman, Ethan. 1998. " 'Applied Idealism': Theodore Roosevelt's Prudent Approach to Conservation." *Theodore Roosevelt Association Journal* 22, no. 3: 3–7.

———. 1997. "The Prudential FDR." In Mark Rozell and William Pederson, eds., *FDR and the Modern Presidency*, 147–65. Westport, CT: Praeger.

———. 1994a. " 'Falling Back' on Natural Law and Prudence: A Reply to Souryal and Potts." *Journal of Criminal Justice Education* 5, no. 2 (Fall): 189–203.

———. 1994b. "Under the Circumstances: Abraham Lincoln and Classical Prudence." In Frank Williams, William Pederson, and Vincent Marsala, eds., *Abraham Lincoln: Sources and Styles of Leadership*, 3–15. Westport, CT: Greenwood Press.

Flexner, James. 1974. *Washington: The Indispensable Man*. Boston: Little, Brown and Co.

Freeman, Douglas S. 1968. *Washington*. New York: Charles Scribner's Sons.

Freidel, Frank. 1990. *Franklin D. Roosevelt: A Rendezvous with Destiny*. Boston: Little, Brown and Co.

Garver, Eugene. 1987. *Machiavelli and the History of Prudence*. Madison: University of Wisconsin Press.

George, Alexander. 1974. "Assessing Presidential Character." *World Politics* 26, no. 2: 234–82.

Gibbs, Nancy. 1998. "Outrageous Fortune." *Time*. March 30, pp. 21–25.

Gibbs, Nancy, and Michael Duffy. 1998. " 'I Misled People.' " *Time*, August 31, pp. 27–35.

Goodwin, Doris Kearns. 1994. *No Ordinary Time*. New York: Simon and Schuster.

Gough, Russell. 1998. "The Irony of Clinton Talking about Character." *Mobile Register*. July 10, p. 13A.

Greenhouse, Linda. 1999. "In His Opinion." *New York Times Book Review*, September 26, p. 14.

Greenstein, Fred. 1982. *The Hidden-Hand Presidency*. New York: Basic Books.

————. 1974. *Children and Politics*. New Haven: Yale University Press.

Gunnell, John. 1986. *Between Philosophy and Politics: The Alienation of Political Theory*. Amherst: University of Massachusetts Press.

Hallowell, John. 1963. *The Moral Foundation of Democracy*. Chicago: University of Chicago Press.

————. 1950. *Main Currents in Modern Political Thought*. New York: Holt, Rinehart and Winston.

Hallowell, John, and Jene Porter. 1997. *Political Philosophy: The Search for Humanity and Order*. Scarborough, Ontario: Prentice Hall Canada Inc.

Harbaugh, William H. 1975. *The Life and Times of Theodore Roosevelt*. New York: Oxford University Press.

Hargrove, Erwin. 1998. *The President as Leader: Appealing to the Better Angels of Our Nature*. Lawrence: University Press of Kansas.

Herring, Pendleton. 1965. *The Politics of Democracy*. New York: W. W. Norton and Co.

Hirsch, E. D. 1987. *Cultural Literacy*. Boston: Houghton Mifflin.

Hirschfield, Robert, ed. 1982. *The Power of the Presidency*. New York: Aldine Publishing Co.

Hobbes, Thomas. 1962. *Leviathan*. Edited by Michael Oakeshott. New York: Collier Books.

Hoekstra, Douglas. 1989. "Neustadt, Barber and Presidential Statesmanship: The Problem of Lincoln." *Presidential Studies Quarterly* 19, no. 2: 184–99.

Hofstadter, Richard. 1961. *The American Political Tradition*. New York: Vintage Books.

Hughes, Emmet John. 1973. *The Living Presidency*. New York: Coward, McCann and Geoghegan.

————. 1963. *The Ordeal of Power*. New York: Atheneum.

Jaffa, Harry. 1982. *Crisis of the House Divided*. Chicago: University of Chicago Press.

James, William. 1950. "What Pragmatism Means." In Gail Kennedy, ed., *Pragmatism and American Culture*, pp. 1–23. Boston: D. C. Heath and Co.

Johnson, Haynes. 1964. *The Bay of Pigs*. New York: W. W. Norton and Co.

Johnson, Haynes, and David Broder. 1996. *The System*. Boston: Little, Brown and Co.

Key, V. O. 1967. *Parties, Politics and Pressure Groups*. New York: Thomas Y. Crowell.

Knebel, Fletcher, and Charles Bailey II. 1960. *No High Ground*. Westport, CT: Greenwood Press.

Koenig, Louis. 1996. *The Chief Executive*. New York: Harcourt Brace.

Korematsu v. United States, 323 U.S. 214 (1944).

Kramer, Michael. 1993. "Don't Settle for Hypocrisy." *Time*, July 26, p. 41.

Lester, Will. 1998. "Poll: Starr More Believable." *Mobile Register.* September 13, pp. 1A, 4A.
Levy, Leonard. 1963. *Jefferson and Civil Liberties: The Darker Side.* Cambridge, MA: Harvard University Press.
Levy, Michael. 1988. "Political Theory and the Emergence of a Policy Science." In Edward Portis and Michael Levy, eds., *Handbook of Political Theory and Policy Science*, 1–10. Westport, CT: Greenwood Press.
Lippmann, Walter. 1955. *The Public Philosophy.* New York: New American Library.
Lipset, Seymour Martin. 1979. *The First New Nation.* New York: W. W. Norton.
Locke, John. 1974. "Two Treatises of Government." In Ernest Barker, ed., *The Social Contract*, 3–143. New York: Oxford University Press.
Maas, Peter. 1973. *Serpico.* New York: Viking.
Machiavelli, Niccolo. 1992. *The Prince.* Edited and translated by Robert Adams. New York: W. W. Norton.
Madison, James, Alexander Hamilton, and John Jay. 1961. *The Federalist Papers.* Edited by Clinton Rossiter. New York: Mentor Books.
Malone, Dumas, and Basil Rauch. 1965. *America and World Leadership.* New York: Appleton-Century-Crofts.
———. 1960a. *The Republic Comes of Age.* New York: Appleton-Century-Crofts.
———. 1960b. *The New Nation.* New York: Appleton-Century-Crofts.
———. 1960c. *Crisis of the Union.* New York: Appleton-Century-Crofts.
Maney, Patrick. 1992. *The Roosevelt Presence.* New York: Twayne Publishers.
Mansfield, Harvey, Jr. 1993. *Taming the Prince.* Baltimore: Johns Hopkins University Press.
Maritain, Jacques. 1951. *Man and the State.* Chicago: University of Chicago Press.
McCullough, David. 1992. *Truman.* New York: Simon and Schuster.
McDonald, Forrest. 1994. *The American Presidency.* Lawrence: University Press of Kansas.
Miller, Merle. 1974. *Plain Speaking: An Oral Biography of Harry Truman.* New York: Berkley.
Morgan, Edmund. 1980. *The Genius of George Washington.* New York: W. W. Norton.
Morgenthau, Hans. 1967. *Scientific Man versus Power Politics.* Chicago: University of Chicago Press.
———. 1966. *Politics among Nations.* New York: Alfred A. Knopf.
Morison, Elting E., ed. 1952. *The Letters of Theodore Roosevelt.* Volume 6. Cambridge, MA: Harvard University Press.
Moskop, Wynne. 1996. "Prudence as a Paradigm for Political Leaders." *Political Psychology.* 17, no. 4: 619–41.

Mulgan, R. G. 1977. *Aristotle's Political Theory*. New York: Oxford University Press.

Myer, Dillon. 1972. *Uprooted Americans*. Tucson: University of Arizona Press.

Nagel, Paul. 1997. *John Quincy Adams*. New York: Alfred A. Knopf.

Neustadt, Richard. 1990. *Presidential Power*. 3d ed. New York: The Free Press.

———. 1980. *Presidential Power*. 2d ed. New York: John Wiley & Sons, Inc.

Nevins, Allan. 1932. *Grover Cleveland: A Study in Courage*. Volume 1. New York: Dodd, Mead & Co.

Niebuhr, Reinhold. 1944. *The Children of Light and the Children of Darkness*. New York: Charles Scribner's Sons.

———. 1941. *The Nature and Destiny of Man*. Volume 1. New York: Charles Scribner's Sons.

———. 1932. *Moral Man and Immoral Society*. New York: Charles Scribner's Sons.

Nixon, Richard. 1978. *RN: The Memoirs of Richard Nixon*. New York: Grosset and Dunlap.

Nussbaum, Martha. 1994. *The Therapy of Desire*. Princeton, NJ: Princeton University Press.

———. 1986. *The Fragility of Goodness: Luck and Ethics in Greek Tragedy and Philosophy*. Cambridge: Cambridge University Press.

Oakeshott, Michael. 1967. "Learning and Teaching." In R. S. Peters, ed., *The Concept of Education*, 156–76. London: Routledge and Kegan Paul.

Osgood, Robert. 1965. *Ideals and Self-Interest in America's Foreign Relations*. Chicago: University of Chicago Press.

Oshinsky, David. 1985. *A Conspiracy So Immense*. New York: The Free Press.

Perkins, Frances. 1946. *The Roosevelt I Knew*. New York: Viking Press.

Peterson, Merrill. 1970. *Thomas Jefferson and the New Nation*. New York: Oxford University Press.

Pieper, Josef. 1959. *The Four Cardinal Virtues*. New York: Harcourt, Brace & World.

Pious, Richard. 1996. *The Presidency*. Boston: Allyn and Bacon.

Polanyi, Michael. 1967. *The Tacit Dimension*. New York: Anchor Books.

Pooley, Eric. 1998. "Meanwhile, Back in Arkansas . . ." *Time*, April 13, pp. 48–49.

Randall, J. G. 1945. *Lincoln the President*. Volume 1. New York: Dodd, Mead and Co.

Rauschning, Hermann. 1939. *The Revolution of Nihilism*. London: William Heinemann, Ltd.

Riordan, William. 1963. *Plunkitt of Tammany Hall*. New York: Dutton.

Roosevelt, Theodore. 1952. "TR to Harry Hamilton Johnston." In Elting Morison, ed., *The Letters of Theodore Roosevelt*. Volume 6, p. 1125. Cambridge, MA: Harvard University Press.

————. 1913. *An Autobiography*. New York: The Macmillan Co.

Ross, W. D. 1960. *Aristotle*. New York: Meridian Books.

Rousseau, Jean-Jacques. 1978. *On the Social Contract*. Edited by Roger Masters. Translated by Judith Masters. New York: St. Martin's Press.

Rovere, Richard. 1967. *Senator Joe McCarthy*. Cleveland: World Publishing Co.

Ruderman, Richard. 1997. "Aristotle and the Recovery of Political Judgment." *American Political Science Review* 91, no. 2: 409–20.

Russell, Francis. 1968. *The Shadow of Blooming Grove*. New York: McGraw-Hill.

Ryan, Alan. 1999. "The Revival of Pragmatism." *New York Times Book Review*, April 4, p. 10.

San Antonio School District v. Rodriguez, 411 U.S. 1 (1973).

Sandel, Michael. 1988. "The Political Theory of the Procedural Republic." In Robert Reich, ed., *The Power of Public Ideas*, 110–21. Cambridge, MA: Ballinger Publishing Company.

Schell, Jonathan. 1975. *The Time of Illusion*. New York: Vintage Books.

Schlesinger, Arthur, Jr. 1996. "The Ultimate Approval Rating." *New York Times Magazine*, December 15, pp. 47–51.

————. 1973. *The Imperial Presidency*. Boston: Houghton Mifflin.

————. 1967. *A Thousand Days*. Greenwich, CT: Fawcett Crest.

————. 1960. *The Politics of Upheaval*. Boston: Houghton Mifflin.

————. 1958. *The Coming of the New Deal*. Boston: Houghton Mifflin.

Sherwood, Robert. 1950. *Roosevelt and Hopkins*. New York: Harper and Brothers.

Shogan, Robert. 1999. *The Double-Edged Sword*. Boulder, CO: Westview Press.

Sigmund, Paul, ed. 1988. *St. Thomas Aquinas on Politics and Ethics*. New York: W. W. Norton and Company.

Skowronek, Stephen. 1993. *The Politics Presidents Make*. Cambridge, MA: Harvard University Press.

Smith, Wayne. 1987. *The Closest of Enemies*. New York: W. W. Norton and Co.

Solomon, John. 1998. "Starr Reports Sex Details; White House Fights Back." *Mobile Register*, September 12, pp. 1A, 4A.

Sorensen, Theodore. 1966. *Kennedy*. New York: Bantam Books.

Stoler, Mark. 1989. *George C. Marshall*. Boston: Twayne Publishers.

Strauss, Leo. 1965. *Natural Right and History*. Chicago: University of Chicago Press.

Szilard, Leo. 1960. "President Truman Did Not Understand." *U.S. News and World Report*. August 15, pp. 68–71.

Szulc, Tad. 1986. *Fidel*. New York: Avon Books.

Tackett, Michael. 2000. "Voters Embrace Sinners over Saints." *Mobile Register*. January 30, pp. D1, D4.

Thobaben, Robert, Donna Schlagheck, and Charles Funderburk. 1998. *Issues in American Political Life*. Upper Saddle River, NJ: Prentice-Hall.

Thomas, Norman, Joseph Pika, and Richard Watson. 1994. *The Politics of the Presidency*. Washington, DC: Congressional Quarterly Press.

Thompson, Kenneth. 1956. "The Political Philosophy of Reinhold Niebuhr." In Charles Kegley and Robert Bretall, eds., *Reinhold Niebuhr: His Religious, Social, and Political Thought*, 152–75. New York: Macmillan.

Thucydides. 1951. *The Peloponnesian War*. Edited by John Finley, Jr. New York: The Modern Library.

Tocqueville, Alexis de. 1969. *Democracy in America*. Edited by J. P. Mayer. Translated by George Lawrence. New York: Anchor Books.

Towell, Pat. 1993a. "Months of Hope, Anger, Anguish Produce Policy Few Admire." *Congressional Quarterly* (July 24): 1966–71.

———. 1993b. "Congress Reinforces Gay Ban as Court Assaults Continue." *Congressional Quarterly* (November 20): 3210–11.

Truman, David. 1971. *The Governmental Process*. New York: Alfred A. Knopf.

Tugwell, Rexford. 1957. *The Democratic Roosevelt*. Garden City, NY: Doubleday.

Tulis, Jeffrey. 1987. *The Rhetorical Presidency*. Princeton, NJ: Princeton University Press.

———. 1981. "On Presidential Character." In Joseph Bessette and Jeffrey Tulis, eds., *The Presidency in the Constitutional Order*, 283–313. Baton Rouge: Louisiana State University Press.

United States v. Carolene Products Co., 304 U.S. 144 (1938).

Walworth, Arthur. 1969. *Woodrow Wilson*. Baltimore: Penguin Books.

White, Theodore. 1975. *Breach of Faith*. New York: Atheneum.

Williams, T. Harry. 1953. "Abraham Lincoln: Principle and Pragmatism in Politics." *Mississippi Valley Historical Review* 40, no. 1: 89–106.

Wilson, R. L. 1971. *Theodore Roosevelt: Outdoorsman*. New York: Winchester Press.

Wyden, Peter. 1984. *Day One*. New York: Simon and Schuster.

Index

About the Author

ETHAN M. FISHMAN is Professor of Political Science at the University of South Alabama. His research deals with the application of classical Western concepts to American politics. Among his publications are *Likely Stories: Essays on Political Philosophy and Contemporary American Fiction*, *Public Policy and the Public Good*, and *George Washington: Foundation of Presidential Leadership and Character* edited with Mark Rozell and William Pederson.